NO[illegible] AS A THIEF

A Historic Premillennial Perspective on the Rapture

Reginald C. Kimbro

ISBN: 1505364949
ISBN-13: 978-1505364941

DEDICATION

I want to dedicate this book to the memory of the men of the Free Presbyterian Church of Scotland who studied under Thomas Chalmers during the mid-19th century and supplied such a rich heritage of reverent and Reformed comment upon Holy Scripture, so many of whom were premillennial while still maintaining a strong commitment to historic Covenant Theology. May the Lord raise up another such like minded generation.

CONTENTS

ACKNOWLEDGMENTS

I want to thank Derrick Bowman, my Associate Minister, for his skillful work in the layout and artwork for the book. I also want to thank parishioner and friend Kevin Hamilton and my mother Barbara Kimbro for their careful labors in proofreading.

While significant additions and alterations appear in the present book, the core of the work first appeared as a research thesis for the MTh degree from the Wales Evangelical School of Theology. I thank my supervisor Dr. Robert Letham for his patience and helpful suggestions along the way.

INTRODUCTION

Best-sellers don't often emerge from within the Christian community. But when they do, it's usually not the result of the publication of a careful exegetical commentary on Romans or a conservative Pauline study. (Contrary to this writer's wishes, demand remains low for the reprint of James Buchanan's classic 19th century work on *The Doctrine of Justification,* and it goes in and out of short run printings). But best-sellers, even by *New York Times* standards, have emerged from the field of Christian prophecy. From Hal Lindsay's mega hit *The Late Great Planet Earth* in 1970 to the Tim Lahay/Jerry Jenkins *Left Behind* series of more recent years, which sold in the tens of millions, there seems to be no lull in the appetite for the Dispensational pre-tribulational version of prophecy. The *Left Behind* series has spawned several feature films; first a trilogy of films starring the Evangelical Christian Kurt Cameron beginning in 2000, and in 2014 another featuring Hollywood A-Lister Nicolas Cage. To be fair, one should note that not all proponents of the pre-tribulation Rapture support the popular and enhanced fictional accounts displayed in the novels and movies. They rightly fear that these could take away from the credibility of an important Biblical teaching. But that doesn't change the fact that a huge appetite for these stories exists and that many Christians and Christian leaders indeed view them as worthy evangelistic tools.

The Rapture and the Tribulation have not only captivated the interests of the Evangelical church in North America but the popular teaching on the subject has substantially impacted society at large. This compelled one secular observer to conclude, "The rapture is woven into the fabric of American culture."[1] The man on the street might not know much about the Person and work of Christ, but he probably knows something about the Rapture. I was impressed several years ago during the U.S. presidential campaign of the year 2000 to hear the celebrated conservative radio talk show host Rush Limbaugh criticizing the Democratic candidate Al Gore, who in a speech the previous day had properly used the term "rapture" to denote an experience of great joy or enthusiasm. Limbaugh seemed amazed and rebuked Vice-President Gore for using language connected with "the end of the world." Whether the usually astute Limbaugh spoke out of sarcasm or out of ignorance of the basic meaning of the word is irrelevant. He knew his vast audience would make the connection with Christianity's specialized usage of the word.

---

[1] Amy Johnson Frykholm, *Rapture Culture: Left Behind in Evangelical America* (New York: Oxford University Press, 2004), 13.

The overwhelming success of pre-tribulationism within the North American church, propelled perhaps equally by the devotion of its adherents and the dogmatism of its proponents, certainly accounts for this situation in the broader culture. Beginning with the teachings of John Nelson Darby in the Brethren churches during the mid-19th century, the doctrine grew beyond that limited sphere and came into its own during the prophetic conference movement of the late 19th and early 20th centuries. It is indeed remarkable that from that relatively recent introduction this version of end times events has gained the exposure and explosive popularity that it has. But is this popular view of the Rapture clearly spelled out in scripture? How much actual evidence does the Bible provide to support the conclusion that believers will be taken away before the Tribulation of the last days comes upon the world? The following study seeks to provide a charitable challenge to this popular doctrine and concludes that evidence for this deliverance of the church from that "time of Jacob's trouble" is lacking and that believers will in fact be present during those trying years that will come upon the earth.

For those familiar with the Rapture debate, I should state at the outset that I am a committed premillennialist in my understanding of Biblical prophecy, so I am going to agree with pre-tribulationists on a lot of points. We will even agree (contrary to much teaching within the pre-tribulational camp suggesting otherwise), on our view of how to approach and interpret the Bible's prophetic texts. I am not, however, a proponent of the Dispensational theology that undergirds the pre-tribulational view of the Rapture. The importance of these facts will become evident as the book progresses.

I also wish to point out that I believe there are many more important matters for the Lord's people to be concerned about at the present time—the aforementioned doctrine of justification not the least among them. Important details of the gospel have suffered from neglect and denial in the modern church. Legalism and Phariseeism have reared their heads in conservative circles, while on the other hand lifestyle choices within the professing church have taken a decidedly worldly turn, and genuine Antinomianism has boldly presented itself as well. Evangelical circles are struggling with some of the same debates over fundamental doctrines that caused the Evangelicals to separate from Liberalism a century ago. These are not insignificant problems. I will offer some comments about how the Rapture doctrine affects other doctrines and current issues along the way, but suffice it to say that I believe for many reasons, even in the current climate, this subject is worthy of renewed study, if for no other reason than the fact that it does garner attention and that it can serve, as it did in my life, as a springboard to generate interest in the study of other more important matters.

I should include a note concerning the obvious. This book is an argument—an argument attempting to prove that the scriptures do not support the popular teaching of a pre-tribulation Rapture. Argument (or debate) is something that believers should be able to pursue with other believers without being argumentative, especially on matters of lesser importance such as this point of detail in a prophetic chart. We have to agree to disagree with our brethren on many points as we study the details of scripture. Hopefully we can do so with charity. Let us just weigh the relative importance of those disagreements. During the 20th century, however, few doctrines were held with more rigidity or maintained as matters of necessary separation within churches and religious organizations than was pre-tribulationism. While this still characterizes many circles, there is hope that a less dogmatic spirit prevails in the hearts of some pre-tribulationists today, and that such a spirit will be found within the readers of these pages.

I belong to a denomination which throughout its history has allowed liberty on many details of eschatology (the study of "last things"). I have dear friends and colleagues with whom I work very closely that do not agree with me on the larger detail of the millennium itself. We do so with mutual understanding, love, and respect. We also do so with a firm commitment to the belief that details become more important and unity becomes more essential when the church approaches the subjects surrounding the doctrine of salvation (soteriology). Interestingly, this eschatological liberty has not produced an apathetic spirit with reference to prophecy as some might believe. Rather, I have known few men who are better versed in the area of prophetic study than some of my denominational colleagues. So I open this book with a plea for charity in the larger body of Christ, to which these words are addressed, and I ask at least for patience and grace in the minds of any pre-tribulationists who may choose to read these pages. I will seek to be objective and charitable in my presentation. My arguments will be pointed at times, but I will endeavor never to misrepresent my opponents. Those who may not share my premillennial viewpoint on the broader understanding of end time events should note that for the sake of argument this book will assume without debate many points of that prophetic outline that are indeed worthy of serious discussion and challenge in other contexts, but this book focuses on the timing of the Rapture within the premillennial system.

The following pages are a brief presentation of the Rapture debate from a simple perspective. My design is not so much to convince everyone of my particular viewpoint as to inform and awaken those within pre-tribulationism to the fact that other credible viewpoints on the details of prophecy do exist among serious and conservative students of scripture. And in the event that the pre-tribulational Rapture proves not to be an accurate representation of the Biblical doctrine, it may perhaps be salutary to have at least considered the possibility that all believers will remain upon the earth during those days.

Chapter 1

SOME CURRENT AFFAIRS IN THE CHURCH AND A PROPHETIC OVERVIEW

A study of the Rapture involves many questions from the broader field of prophetic interpretation and even some important questions from other areas of doctrine. Obviously a book of this size cannot adequately address all of these connected issues, but a few brief thoughts on some general matters of history, particularly dealing with the current situation in the church in North America, and the broader questions of prophecy in general might be helpful to lay some groundwork.

While there certainly are matters of great significance that arise between the competing millennial perspectives on prophecy, historically many segments of the church have maintained a charity within their ranks when it comes to disagreement on these details when agreement exists on the major points of doctrine concerning the end. These bedrock prophetic doctrines include:

1. Christ's visible, bodily return to the earth.
2. The resurrection of both the righteous and the unrighteous.
3. The new heavens and the new earth.
4. The eternal state, including the doctrines of eternal bliss for the redeemed and of eternal punishment for the lost—i.e. the doctrines of heaven and hell.

These doctrines comprise a bare minimum of orthodox expectation concerning the future.

Unlike those who have allowed liberty on the details of prophecy, Pre-tribulational circles elevated the subject of prophecy to a higher position. Prophetic questions became matters of separation. The groups allowing liberty on prophetic details, especially those adhering to the major Reformed Confessions, have, however, usually required this level of unity on the details of the doctrine of salvation. With the advent of Dispensationalism this situation was uniquely reversed in institutions which embraced the new theology. These institutions insisted upon uniformity on prophetic details. The pre-tribulation Rapture became a benchmark. Completing the contrast in a remarkable way, these circles often paid less attention to the details of the doctrine of salvation and either wittingly or unwittingly allowed a great diversity of opinion on those details to coexist within their ranks. In more recent decades, when this soteriological deficiency gathered notice, controversy entered Dispensational circles as adherents began to struggle for soteriological identity. As a major illustration of this reality, a debate known as the "Lordship Salvation" controversy erupted within Dispensational ranks in the latter decades of the twentieth century—a controversy which continues in various forms to the present day. In that debate, significant disagreement appears concerning the very nature of what it means to be a true Christian and the Dispensational system has not been able to decide the question.[2] In addition to, but not unrelated to that debate, local churches with Dispensational heritage now frequently struggle or even reach a point of division when younger ministers, influenced by the returning influence of Reformed theology, begin to investigate the details of the doctrine of salvation. Granted, men embracing Calvinism while ministering within Dispensational circles have frequently made a lot of noise in the process and caused unnecessary strife or division, but the fact is that even the most diplomatic of ministers often has a

---

[2] For a fuller discussion of the important issues surrounding Dispensational theology see, John Gerstner, *Wrongly Dividing the Word of Truth* (Morgan, Pennsylvania: Soli Deo Gloria, 2000); Reginald C. Kimbro, *The Gospel According to Dispensationalism* (Toronto: Wittenburg Publications, 1995); Keith Matthison, *Rightly Dividing the People of God?* (Philipsburg, New Jersey: Presbyterian and Reformed, 1995).

lot on his plate when he comes to realize that he presides over a church that is *already divided* over the details of the most important doctrine of all. If he is going to revisit the vital doctrines of the gospel in the modern context he must confront this reality. He has not caused the division. He has merely been left to expose a division that has existed for a long time.

This contemporary situation highlights a truth that is perhaps unwelcome but some are now willing to address. Dispensationalism as a whole has fallen upon difficult times. Arising in the midst of this reality, the movement called "Progressive Dispensationalism" has admittedly[3] opened doors for the Rapture debate to reemerge in the coming days for a broader audience. This is due, no doubt, to the major challenges which the framers of Progressive Dispensationalism have brought to the entire Dispensational system. These scholars have, while within Dispensational institutions, abandoned the fundamental premise of Dispensational theology—the dissociation of Israel and the NT church. The significance of this for the Rapture debate will become apparent as the following study unfolds.

From another perspective, one should pause to contrast the Bible conference movements of the early part of the last century with those of the early part of this century. In the early 20th century, Bible conferences focused heavily upon

---

[3] See Robert L. Saucy, *The Case for Progressive Dispensationalism* (Grand Rapids: Zondervan, 1993), 8-9.

prophecy and pre-tribulationism became dominant in the North American church. Popular 21st century conferences have focused attention on matters closely related to the doctrine of salvation and most of the major conference speakers adhere to the Reformed faith, in contrast to those who were either already outside or who departed from the Reformed tradition as they embraced Dispensationalism a century ago. While significant sections of Evangelicalism still do not embrace Reformed theology (and notably, pre-tribulational circles are representative in that regard), the church has nonetheless reached a point historically where an objective evaluation of the Rapture question may find a greater hearing than it has for several decades. Such a hope lies underneath this book.

One final historical observation deserves mention. The position argued in this book, Historic Premillennialism, still struggles to gain a large audience in these times of theological transition. There may be many reasons for this, but there are some observations that merit attention. This may not reflect a scientific poll, but one is compelled to observe that of the many leaders who left Dispensationalism over the past half century and embraced Reformed theology few retained a premillennial position. Could not more of them have objectively examined the premillennial viewpoint and removed from it any details which they deemed to be based upon erroneous Dispensational presuppositions and have arrived at a non-Dispensational Historic

Premillennialism? From the other vantage point, one has to wonder if many who were already ministering in Reformed circles were discouraged from giving premillennialism an objective hearing lest they be wrongly identified with Dispensationalism during those mid-20th century decades of intense debate between the Covenantal and the Dispensational systems. This is an important observation, because for many Evangelical leaders today, it seems that the only reason they still profess to be Dispensational is because they believe that is the only way to be premillennial. This is true of the founders of Progressive Dispensationalism and of such popular teachers as John MacArthur. When one examines their explanations for retaining Dispensationalism he finds that the only thing they defend is premillennialism and the only thing they refute is amillennialism,[4] all the while believing that they have adequately addressed their reasons for rejecting Covenant Theology and retaining a revised version of Dispensationalism that is rid of the serious errors of previous generations. One could be excused for suggesting that many contemporary leaders who claim the title of Dispensationalist are not really Dispensationalists at all, according to historical and theological definition, given the fact that they have abandoned the definitive tenet of Classical Dispensationalism regarding the *dissociation* of

---

[4] For examples of this see Robert Saucy *The Case for Progressive Dispensationalism* (Grand Rapids: Zondervan, 1993), p. 9. Also John MacArthur *Faith Works* (Dallas: Word Publishing, 1993), 219-233.

Israel and the NT church and embraced a view which finds *continuity* existing between the OT and the NT peoples. This certainly highlights the need for a return to historical and theological clarity in dealing with the vitally important topic of systematic theology in the contemporary church.

Leaving these historical observations aside, at this point a brief survey of the views of the millennium may be of help in laying some additional foundation for the present study of the Rapture within the premillennial system.

Recent centuries have witnessed the fine tuning of Evangelical opinion concerning Christian eschatology. While subcategories do appear, three major viewpoints have found a place within the teaching of the church. Named with reference to their understanding of the Second Advent of Christ and its relation to an *earthly* manifestation of the kingdom, these competing perspectives are: premillennialism, amillennialism, and postmillennialism. Premillennialism asserts the coming of Christ will precede the kingdom. There will be a 1000 year reign of Christ on the earth that follows His glorious return. Postmillennialism claims that Christ's return will follow a kingdom age that manifests itself on the earth without Christ's presence. Amillennialism holds that no earthly kingdom occurs after the current New Testament church age but rather that the current church age is the only earthly stage of the kingdom to be expected.

A-millennialism is perhaps an unfortunate and uncharitable title. The prefix in this instance denotes the absence of a 'millennium' when in reality amillennialism does see a kingdom which is currently manifested between the Advents of the Messiah in the experience of the New Testament church which is both international in character and fuller in its possession of the Spirit and power. Those who easily dismiss amillennialism should consider the clear statement of Christ's current *enthronement as David's Son* as accomplished by His resurrection and ascension to the Father's right hand (Acts 2:30-36). Some aspect of the Kingdom has already started. Premillennialists who ignore this put themselves in a difficult position exegetically. In earlier years amillennialism was recognized as a variation or a subset of postmillennialism because the Second Advent actually *follows* the 'kingdom' in this scheme. Justification for the third category rests in the fact that postmillennialism, as it is now distinguished from amillennialism, anticipates an *additional age* to follow the current age, while contrary to both postmillennialism and premillennialism, amillennialism does *not* expect an additional age to follow the present age before the eternal state.

Another important matter surrounding the amillennial system merits additional attention. A question of hermeneutics (the science of Biblical interpretation) presents itself in the debate between amillennialism and the other millennial viewpoints. Since amillennialism views the current church age as the fulfillment of the Old Testament kingdom prophecies, and the current age is an international spiritual kingdom and not a restored kingdom with National Israel at its center, these prophecies must be interpreted 'spiritually' and not 'literally' in the amillennial understanding. This is not an insignificant difference from the other schools of thought. (While this most often surfaces in the debate between premillennialism and amillennialism, this matter of hermeneutics also applies between amillennialism and postmillennialism in some of its forms). The other millennial views expect a 'literal' earthly kingdom flowing from the Old Testament promises to National Israel and amillennialism does not.

A point that is often misunderstood (and in many cases even misrepresented) in this discussion of hermeneutics is the fact that this question of a 'literal' versus a 'spiritual' interpretation of the kingdom passages should be limited to the debate surrounding the millennium and not transferred to the debate between Dispensationalism and Covenant Theology. The millennium, and the hermeneutical questions that surround it, stand as intramural debates among Covenant Theologians. The system of Covenant Theology simply does not dictate which millennial viewpoint its adherents maintain. Dispensational pre-tribulationists, however, have applied this hermeneutical difference between the millennial schools of thought (where it legitimately applies) to the larger debate between themselves and the system of Covenant Theology (where it does not legitimately apply). It became standard fare within Dispensational circles to accuse Covenant Theologians *en masse* as holding to a 'spiritualizing hermeneutic' when it is only the subset of Covenant Theologians who are amillennial to whom the charge accurately applies. (One should also note that this hermeneutical problem applies only to the limited question of the millennium and that amillennialists do not have an entirely different way of viewing the Bible as they, and the whole system of Covenant Theology, are often wrongly accused of by Dispensationalists). This became one of the most unfortunate misunderstandings of the twentieth century. Charles Ryrie is representative when he states categorically:

> The covenant premillennialist...retains the idea of the millennial kingdom, though he finds little support for it in the Old Testament kingdom prophecies since he generally assigns them to the church.[5]

It is not the Covenantal or "Historic Premillennialist" that generally assigns the Old Testament kingdom prophecies to the church, but rather the amillennialist. Covenantal premillennialists can and do look for a future for National Israel in every way that a Dispensationalist does. Even many historical postmillennialists look for the restoration of National Israel as the prelude to the future kingdom age they expect. The present study cannot fully develop this topic, but

[5] *Dispensationalism Today* (Chicago: Moody Press, 1965), 44.

it does expose a misunderstanding that still prevails in the debate between Covenant Theology and Dispensationalism, particularly in the way that Dispensationalists argue their case. It will take a long time for the misunderstanding and misinformation on this topic to be overcome and corrected.

Leaving these larger comments on the amillennial perspective, a few comments on the other viewpoints will complete this brief survey of some basic groundwork. The expectation of an additional age after the current age offers more opportunity for variation within the other systems. Postmillennialists believe that the kingdom will arrive before the Second Advent. This raises the question of what initiates the kingdom. Will it follow a great move of the Spirit of God in revival (with or without reference to National Israel), or will it come to pass through the efforts of the church in successfully replacing other religions and secular powers through tangible means? How should the church pursue this kingdom—through preaching and praying or through social and political activity? Variations on these questions generate intramural debate among postmillennialists and generally represent the older and newer forms of the system.

Within premillennialism, all agree that the Second Advent (Christ's public glorious appearing at the close of the Tribulation period) inaugurates the millennial kingdom, but significant variations within this school of thought arise concerning the Rapture of the church. Will the church be here for all of the Tribulation period, just some of the

Tribulation period, or will it be taken away before the Tribulation period even begins? It is this question within the larger premillennial perspective that this book addresses and thus we move on to the subject at hand. The following chapters seek to provide a simple approach to the question.

Chapter 2

A Simple Approach to the Question

Investigating the time of the Rapture within premillennialism requires a brief statement of definition. The term 'Rapture' does not occur in scripture but has come into theological usage in modern times and appears even in secular dictionaries as "the transporting of believers to heaven at the Second Coming of Christ."[6] One aspect of this particular dictionary definition, however, errs. Not all Christians believe that heaven is the destination of believers after the Rapture. More precisely, the Rapture refers to the taking up of believers to meet Christ "in the air" upon his Second Coming (1 Thess. 4:17). Determining the destination

---

[6] *Oxford Dictionary of English* (Oxford University Press, 2009). Notably this secondary definition appears with the description "North American," which is the segment of the church where Dispensationalism has been most successful.

of believers *following* this meeting of Christ in the air actually requires deciding the central question of this book as it is debated among premillennialists. Some indeed view heaven as the destination of believers following the Rapture. Others believe that the church will return immediately to the earth with Christ as he descends in the Second Advent and establishes the kingdom. So this question of destination is determined by the answer to the question of *when* that meeting in the air occurs.

Refining further, the term Rapture describes a particular aspect of what scripture calls the "first resurrection" (Rev. 20:5-6) which describes the resurrection of believers in distinction from the resurrection of unbelievers. Building from Revelation 20, a distinguishing feature of pre-millennialism stands out in premillennialism's recognition of a temporal separation of the resurrection of the righteous—the "first resurrection"—from the resurrection of the unrighteous—the "rest of the dead." They are separated by the 1000 year millennial reign (Rev. 20:5), which premillennialists take literally. This first resurrection, however, involves two elements. First, those saints who have died are bodily resurrected at this time. They receive their glorified bodies. Secondly, and to the point of definition in the doctrine of the Rapture, believers who are *still living* when the Lord returns are caught up to meet Christ in the air upon His return to the earth with these now resurrected saints. At this point they are "translated" and receive their glorified bodies just as the resurrected saints. As Paul instructs the Corinthians concerning this event, "we shall not all sleep, but we shall all be changed" (1 Cor. 15: 51-53). The changing of this "vile body" that it might be fashioned like his "glorious body" describes that which takes place in believers whose bodies do not need physical resurrection but nonetheless undergo a glorifying transformation at Christ's appearing. Thus while the Rapture involves a physical transportation from earth to the skies to meet Christ in the air (and one should not disregard the significance of this public identification with Christ upon his return), the more significant action is this 'translation'—the change that takes place as these living believers are transformed into Christ's image. As John turns the phrase, "it doth not yet appear what we shall be: but we know that when he shall appear, we shall be like him; for we shall see him as he is" (1John 3:2). As to defining the term "Rapture" then, one finds that it has particular reference to this catching up and *translation of living saints.*

As developed below, the question of the timing of the Rapture concerns its relation to a future period of "Tribulation." Will it be before, during, or after this Tribulation? The opposing schools of thought are thus named: pre-tribulationism, mid-tribulationism, and post-tribulationism. The fact that the destination of believers after the Rapture involves a disagreement between the factions introduces a distinguishing feature of one of the viewpoints.

Post-tribulationism (which is synonymous with what has been called "Historic Premillennialism") holds that after the Rapture the church will immediately return to the earth with Christ as he arrives in the Second Advent at the close of the Tribulation. The other viewpoints all teach that Christ will come to the skies and then return immediately to heaven, taking the church back with him for the whole or whatever part of the Tribulation period remains. Often the varied positions are presented in chart form as Charles Ryrie has done:[7]

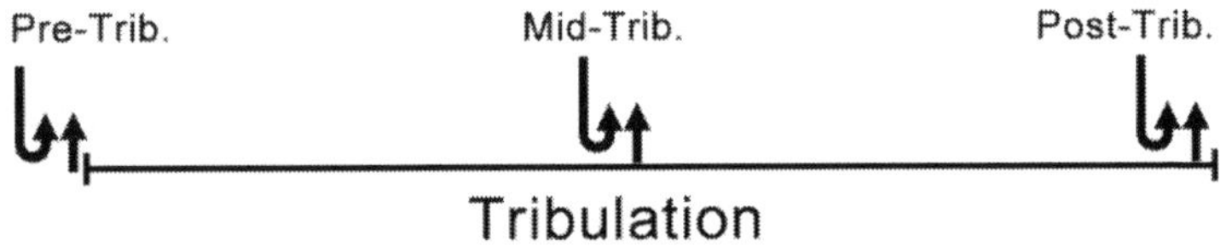

But this does not accurately represent the case. In the case of post-tribulationism the arrow representing a return to the place of origin should belong to the ascending church, not the descending Christ as it does in the other viewpoints. Ryrie commits a common error. The chart should appear:

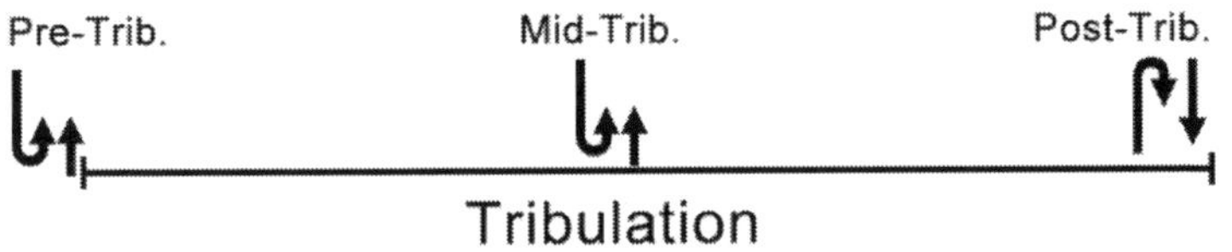

The interpretation of the 70th "week" of Daniel (9:24-27) figures prominently within premillennialism. The

[7] Charles C. Ryrie, *Basic Theology* (Chicago: Moody Press. 1986, 1999), 559.

determination of the seven year duration of the future Tribulation period stems from this prophecy. There is a consensus that the first 69 weeks represent a sequence of 69 seven year periods spanning from the ending of Israel's Babylonian exile to the First Advent of Christ. Most premillennialists understand the "cutting off" of the Messiah at the end of 69 weeks as referring to the crucifixion and Israel's rejection of Jesus.[8] In premillennial interpretation the 70th week does not follow immediately upon the completion of the 69th week. The New Testament church age intervenes and the 70th week begins with the future signing of a covenant between Israel and the "prince that shall come" as described in the prophecy (Daniel 9:26-27). Premillennialism understands this coming prince to be the person scripture elsewhere calls the "Man of Sin" and "Antichrist" (2 Thess. 2: 3; 1 John 2: 18). This deserves emphasis because many pre-tribulationists wrongly assume that the Rapture itself serves to mark the beginning of the Tribulation period, but informed premillennialists of all persuasions agree and recognize that the 70th week is bracketed at the beginning by the signing of this covenant between Israel and the Antichrist, and at the end by the Second Advent. Thus the beginning and ending points of this seven year Tribulation

---

[8] As representative, see B. W. Newton, *Prospects of the Ten Kingdoms of the Roman Empire* (Essex, England: Sovereign Grace Advent Testimony, reprint n.d.), Fourth Edition, 153-164.

period remain unaffected no matter where one places the Rapture.

Historic Premillennialism claims the heritage of the chiliasts (those who believed in the future 1000 year kingdom) in the early church. G. E. Ladd suggests the identical nature of the premillennialism found within some of the early Fathers with what our modern context calls post-tribulationism.[9] Even the notable pre-tribulationist John Walvoord admits that post-tribulationism claims the majority historically within the older premillennialism. He also includes amillennialism and postmillennialism within the "post-tribulational" category because each of these sees the NT church passing through the Tribulation no matter how they define it.[10] The growing popularity of pre-tribulationism surrounding the turn of the 20th century pushed post-tribulationism to the fringes of the emerging Evangelical and Fundamentalist movements. Strong leaders such as C. I. Scofield and A. C. Gaebelein were quite successful in ostracizing their post-tribulational opponents within those early decades. In his historical survey, Reiter notices that a mid-20th century resurgence of post-tribulationism followed a greater commitment to scholarship among Evangelicals though its adherents suffered from this

---

[9] George Eldon Ladd, *The Blessed Hope* (Grand Rapids: Eerdmans, 1956), 18.

[10] John F. Walvoord, *The Rapture Question* (Grand Rapids: Zondervan, 1957), 127.

ostracism and its meager literature was not nearly as well funded or disseminated as its pre-tribulational counterparts.[11]

There is no question that pre-tribulationism still commands a majority among modern premillennialists. This stems from the Dispensationalism that mushroomed in popularity in North America within numerous denominational structures after its introduction through the Brethren movement.[12] Again while the debate surrounding the distinctive tenets of Dispensational theology lies beyond the scope of this investigation, its relevance to the current study is noteworthy because the pre-tribulational version of premillennialism owes its popularity to the new version of distinction that J. N. Darby placed between Israel and the New Testament Church. (See the works cited in footnote 2). While the origin of pre-tribulationism may not stem from Darby (as some comments below will notice), even pre-tribulationists admit that this pre-tribulational version of premillennialism was unknown until Darby's era and that he

---

[11] Richard R. Reiter, "The Development of the Rapture Positions" in *The Rapture: Pre-, Mid-, or Post-Tribulational*? (Grand Rapids: Zondervan Acadamie Books, 1984), 23-25.

[12] J. Barton Payne, *The Theology of the Older Testament* (Grand Rapids: Zondervan, 1962). He states on p. 32: "Plymouth Brethren dispensationalism has been widely popularized, particularly through the notes of the *Scofield Reference Bible*; but until recently it has been without serious scholarly support." Reiter concurs, noting that earlier premillennialists, however, did have credentials. See "Development" 27.

serves as the focal point for its meteoric rise in popularity.[13] Sensing this potential difficulty for pre-tribulationism, Walvoord correctly argues that the absence of a doctrine from earlier periods of church history, while worthy of notice, however, does not prove that such a doctrine is false and he gives the doctrine of the Trinity and its formulation within the early centuries of the Christian era as an example. He suggests that the premillennialism of the early church was simply undeveloped, thus explaining the absence of pre-tribulationism.[14] This, however, fails to establish the continuity he wishes to maintain with pre-tribulationism, for the chiliastic Fathers anticipated the church's enduring suffering under the Beast of Revelation,[15] which is not simply an under-developed form of premillennialism as Walvoord would like to suggest, but rather this is truly incompatible with pre-tribulationism at a key point. The defining feature of pre-tribulationism emphasizes that the church will not be present to endure the reign of the Beast of Revelation at all.

As to the first appearance of pre-tribulationism in church history, one has recently remarked, perhaps

---

[13] Walvoord, *Question*, 52.

[14] Walvoord, *Question*, 52-53.

[15] Schaff states:

> The most striking point in the eschatology of the ante-Nicene age is the prominent chiliasm, or millenarianism, that is the belief of a visible reign of Christ in glory for a thousand years, before the general resurrection and judgment.

humorously, or perhaps better understood as issuing a note of caution, that: "the study of the origins of the secret rapture, and the two-stage coming of Christ, has developed in certain circles into something of a cottage industry."[16] Some early critics of pre-tribulationism even suggested a demonic origin to the theory due to certain supposed visions and charismatic utterances within the revivalist movement of Edward Irving that surrounded the doctrine's first appearance. Darby did have interaction with members of this movement. More measured studies, however, are content to observe the seamless nature of the fit between pre-tribulationism and Darby's innovations regarding the doctrine of the church.[17] Obviously a critic of pre-tribulationism, but after a fair survey of the evidence Katterjohn concludes:

> The first precise statement of the doctrine may never be found. Indeed the idea seems to have grown with

---

Philip Schaff, *History of the Christian Church,* Vol. 2 (Grand Rapids: Erdmans, 1985), 614. The dominance of premillennialism is now disputed. See Charles Hill, *Regnum Caelorum: Patterns of Millennial Thought in Early Christianity* (Grand Rapids: Eerdmans, 2001).

[16] Crawford Gibben, *Rapture Fiction and the Evangelical Crisis* (Darlington, England: Evangelical Press, 2006), 35.

[17]For fuller discussion of the origins of pre-tribulationism see: Daniel P. Fuller, *The Hermeneutics of Dispensationalism* (Chicago, Illinois: Northern Baptist Theological Seminary, diss. 1957), copyright 1966, 53-54; Iain Murray, *The Puritan Hope* (Edinburgh: Banner of Truth, 1971), 200; Gibben, *Rapture,* 27-42;

> the times, coming of age in Darby's system after a shaky adolescence in Irvingism.[18]

The key point in the search for the origins of pre-tribulationism is undoubtedly its recent origin. This does not prove fatal to a doctrine, but it does add a note of caution in giving it consideration.

The history of premillennialism subsequent to the introduction of pre-tribulationism has witnessed frequent disputes and division.[19] Nowhere is this more evident than in the circling of the wagons that occurred in the early twentieth century under the Dispensational leadership of C. I. Scofield and A. C. Gaebelein as mentioned above. After some speakers at the popular Niagara Conference began to question the pre-tribulation Rapture position and embraced the Historic Premillennial, or post-tribulational position, the Niagara conference came to an end. Newer conferences emerged but pre-tribulationists redoubled their efforts and demanded that the leadership of these conferences maintain a uniformly pre-tribulational position. This requirement took deep root and became nothing short of a *shibboleth* in the modern Fundamentalist movement and in many Evangelical circles as well.

---

[18]Arthur D. Katterjohn with Mark Fackler, *The Tribulation People* (Carol Stream, Illinois: Creation House, 1975), 114.

[19] Reiter, "Development,"25-26, 33.

What some refer to as "Mediating Positions"[20] on the Rapture question must receive brief mention.

First, the "Partial Rapture" theory holds that only the "watchful" within the church will be taken away in the Rapture and escape the tribulation. Millard Erickson observes that this theory holds forth the possibility of maintaining a doctrine of imminence as defined and defended by pre-tribulationism, while still recognizing the presence of the church within the Tribulation as post-tribulationism maintains. This seems to be an attempt to take the apparent strengths within the two views and merge them together, but the difficulties that stem from viewing one category of believers as subject to the Tribulation while others are delivered from it have relegated this opinion to a very small minority. This view first appeared c.1852 in Robert Govett, and was defended in the 20th century by G. H. Lang.[21]

A curious novelty appears in the opinion of J. Barton Payne which is called "imminent post-tribulationism." Normal post-tribulationism, viewing the Rapture and the Second Advent as occurring at the same time, cannot maintain a strict imminence since the 70th week of Daniel and its observable details must precede the Advent. Payne avoids this difficulty by holding the preterist position that

---

[20] Millard J. Erickson, *A Basic Guide to Eschatology: Making Sense of the Millennium* (Grand Rapids: Baker Books, 1998), 163.

[21] Erickson, *Guide,* 169.

the 70th week of Daniel is already past, thus the Tribulation may begin and believers remain unaware of the fact (just as believers in repressive nations undergo hardships even now), or it is possible that the Tribulation may be of such a brief duration as to not infringe upon a doctrine of imminence. His position too has gained little acceptance and truly represents a significant departure from traditional premillennialism.

More acceptable to some yet still only claiming a small minority is mid-tribulationism. This mid-20th century variation, held by Norman Harrison and Gleason Archer suggests that the church will be present during the first half of the 70th week but will be taken away before the second half of the week during which, as these suggest, the actual "tribulation" occurs. (It may indeed be true that the first half of the week is not marked by the depths of troubles and persecutions that will prevail during the last half of the week. Many who are not mid-tribulational can and do embrace this understanding of the sequence of events during the week). An even more recent variation of mid-tribulationism was suggested with the publication of Marvin Rosenthal's *Pre-Wrath Rapture of the Church* in 1990.[22] While claiming to present an entirely new perspective, Rosenthal's thesis should be classed as a variation of mid-tribulationism as he

---

[22]Marvin Rosenthal, *The Pre-Wrath Rapture of the Church* (Nashville, Tennessee: Thomas Nelson Publishers, 1990).

simply places the wrath from which the church escapes later in the seven years than his mid-tribulational predecessors and locates it nearer the close of the Tribulation period. In his view the Rapture occurs prior to the "Day of the Lord" which begins at the opening of the 7th seal when the fullness of wrath is poured out upon the earth, but this all still occurs *within* the 70th week so the Rapture also occurs within the 70th week—in his understanding approximately ¾ of the way through.[23] This still represents a mid-tribulational position.

These mediating positions receive little individual attention in the examination which follows. This is partly because of their relative obscurity, but it is also because it is unnecessary to distinguish them in the approach that the following chapters pursue. Other than the more obscure preterist variant of Payne and the partial rapture view, the mid-tribulational alternatives really don't represent a substantial departure from pre-tribulationism (to which, significantly, they are subsequent). In each of these views there is a common denominator that the church will be taken from the earth before the great troubles begin. The question lies only in determining whether the removal of the church before those great troubles requires its removal from the whole seven year period or just part of it. If the main argument contained below proves correct, then all of these views will fall together—each coming short of providing

[23] See Rosenthal, *Pre-Wrath*, 241, etc.

evidence that the church will escape any of that Tribulation period.

At this point I want to introduce a straightforward approach to investigating the question. The simple thesis of this book is that the Rapture of the church occurs at the Second Advent of Christ. This is Historic Premillennialism. To begin, it will perhaps be helpful to provide a simple chart. Premillennialism includes the following elements (without including the Rapture on this chart):

At the risk of laboring the obvious, I want to pause and point out that *all* premillennialists agree that the Second Advent occurs at the close of the Tribulation and ushers in the millennial kingdom. (In fact this can be illustrated by pointing out the specific terminology involved. Whenever writers use the term “Second Advent” it always refers to the appearing of Christ in glory to destroy the Man of Sin and establish the millennial reign. This is at the close of the 70th week. When the more generic term “Second Coming” is used, the context will have to determine whether the writer is referring to the Rapture or the Second Advent). This is foundational to all forms of premillennialism. It is Christ’s visible coming in power and great glory that destroys the Man of Sin, redeems Israel from her time of trouble, and establishes the long promised kingdom. Since scripture clearly teaches that the Rapture occurs at the coming of Christ, the proponents of each position except the post-tribulational position must argue for an *additional* coming of Christ prior to the Second Advent. Post-tribulationists teach that the coming of Christ referenced in the Rapture passages is the same coming of Christ as the Second Advent—there is only one Second Coming. *The burden of proof then falls to all premillennialists, except the post-tribulationists, to establish scriptural evidence for an additional coming of Christ.*

Some attempt to avoid this difficulty by claiming the Rapture is not truly a "coming," since in their scheme Christ does not come all the way to the earth but stops in the skies. But this effort to avoid the difficulty proves futile because the language of scripture clearly refers to this event when believers are gathered to him as his "coming" (John 14: 3; 2Thess. 2:1). The other Rapture passages consistently affirm the same.

Another question that perhaps carries little weight, but nonetheless may occur to the serious inquirer, is the question as to why a pre-tribulation Rapture necessitates the *coming* of Christ at all if the purpose of the Rapture is merely to remove the NT church from the earth before the Tribulation. On the pre-tribulational scheme there is no *revelation* of Christ to the world at the time of the Rapture. Although significantly, by contrast, it is the "revelation" of Christ (*apokalupsin:* a word that means to "make known" or to "uncover what was previously hidden") that the Corinthian church was said to be waiting for (1 Cor. 1:7). Why does he not just take the church away? There is no need for Christ to come here merely to return immediately to heaven. He can easily bring the church to heaven from heaven. Though it has passed somewhat from popular usage, and was often used by critics of the theory, the title "Secret Rapture" served to highlight the clandestine nature of Christ's "coming" according to pre-tribulationism. The "blessed hope," however, is described in scripture as "the *glorious appearing* of the great God and our Saviour Jesus Christ" (Titus 2:13). Here the word for the "appearing" is *epiphania*, a word which Thayer's lexicon describes as "often used by the Greeks of a glorious manifestation of the gods, and *especially of their advent to help*"(emphasis added). This description of the hope of the church fits better with the Second Advent than with an event witnessed only by those who are removed from the earth while the rest of the earth, without experiencing any revelation of this great God, is left to continue on its course.

While this approach to the question is indeed simple, it is not simplistic. The very nature of the argument hinges on whether or not there is a reason found in the scriptures to conclude that Christ comes to the skies at another point in time prior to his coming at the close of the Tribulation. The burden of proof falls clearly on all the viewpoints except the post-tribulational. This is not a question of where to place one coming among those who disagree as to when that one coming will occur. It is a question of establishing two comings in the case of everyone except the post-tribulationist who holds that the Rapture occurs at the one coming which everyone already agrees occurs at the close of the Tribulation.

In an attempt to deflect this difficulty for the pre-tribulational viewpoint and hold post-tribulationism to the same requirement of two future comings, Richard Mayhue offers the following amazing suggestion:

> No matter what rapture position one holds, Christ's second coming is one event which occurs in two parts—Christ coming in the air to rapture the church and Christ coming to earth to conquer, judge, and set up His kingdom. [24]

His effort to share this problem with post-tribulationism is ingenious but unconvincing. The fact that two or more things happen at the same time simply does not necessitate an additional coming or even two or more "stages" of the one coming. Post-tribulationism maintains one future coming. All of the other viewpoints necessitate two.

Probing this burden of proof and weighing the evidence for an additional coming supplies a major focus of this investigation. Since the pre-tribulational arguments are the most prevalent and the mid-tribulational variations make

---

[24] Richard Mayhue, "Why A Pretribulational Rapture," *The Masters Seminary Journal* 13/2 (Fall 2002), 250.

use of key parts of pre-tribulationism for their argumentation, the bulk of the following survey focuses upon the pre- and post-tribulational debate.

Chapter 3

THE RAPTURE AND THE RESURRECTION

Proposing an additional coming of Christ carries with it the weighty necessity of other duplications, indeed the multiplication of some events. This will become more evident as the examination progresses. At this juncture, however, one key focal point merits attention before scrutinizing the evidence suggested for the additional coming. Alexander Reese builds his opening argument for post-tribulationism upon an observation from three major texts describing the Rapture: [25]

> *"...I will come again and receive you unto myself..." (John 14:3)*

[25] Alexander Reese, *The Approaching Advent of Christ* (Grand Rapids: Grand Rapids International Publications, 1975 reprint), 34-94.

> *"Now we beseech you, brethren, by the coming of our Lord Jesus Christ, and by our gathering together unto him..." (2 Thess. 2:1)*
>
> *"Then we which are alive and remain shall be caught up together with them in the clouds, to meet the Lord in the air: and so shall we ever be with the Lord." (1 Thess. 4:17)*

Each of these texts clearly references the Rapture. They describe the event as being "received unto" Christ at his "coming again", as being "gathered unto him" at his "coming," and as "meeting the Lord in the air" when he "descend[s] from heaven with a shout, with the voice of the archangel." Each then, places the Rapture at Christ's coming. However the more detailed passage and perhaps the most significant single text describing the Rapture of the church, 1 Thess. 4:17, gives an additional piece of information. *The Rapture will coincide with the resurrection of the righteous dead.*

Paul was seeking to inform and comfort the questioning Thessalonians concerning believers in Christ who had already died. What would their relationship be to Christ when he returned? Paul seems to indicate that the Thessalonians were well versed in their understanding of the fact that they were awaiting the Second Coming but a question arose concerning believers who died before Christ returned. He did not want them to be ignorant about the departed saints. They needed to know that those who had died in Christ will not miss out on that day that the

Thessalonians so eagerly expected. They will be resurrected at that time. This proves highly significant. The resurrection of dead saints and the translation of living saints (the Rapture) will occur *together*. Beyond the coming of Christ, then, we have another point of reference in seeking the timing of the Rapture. Any passages of scripture which give information on the timing of the resurrection of the saints, will also shed light on the timing of the Rapture. A survey of passages that speak of the resurrection of the righteous is therefore of utmost importance in any study of the Rapture.

Isaiah's "Mini-Apocalypse" (24-27)

Premillennialists agree that this portion of Isaiah describes the future restoration of Israel that will occur at the Second Advent. The reader finds that the resurrection of the dead becomes a major expectation within this restoration. Two texts from the prophecy draw particular attention to this event:

> *He will swallow up death in victory; and the Lord will wipe away tears from off all faces; and the rebuke of his people shall he take away from off all the earth: for the Lord hath spoken it (25:8).*

While this verse does not make explicit mention of bodily resurrection, the Apostle Paul's citation of the passage and his reference to its fulfillment in 1 Corinthians 15:54 (where he speaks of this "corruptible" putting on "incorruption," and this "mortal" putting on "immortality") confirms without question that the resurrection is what the prophet has in view.

As this section of the prophecy reaches its climax, however, explicit reference to the resurrection does appear. One reads later:

> *Thy dead men shall live, together with my dead body shall they arise. Awake and sing, ye that dwell in dust: for thy dew is as the dew of herbs, and the earth shall cast out the dead (26: 19).*

The significance of this prophecy for the present study becomes plain. The victory described by the Prophet will include the bodily resurrection of the Lord's people. But when will this event take place? The millennial nature of the prophecy and the timing of this victory plainly appear when one reads, "then shall the moon be confounded, and the sun ashamed, *when the Lord of hosts shall reign in Mount Zion gloriously*" (24:23). The passage therefore reveals a significant detail—the coincidence of the resurrection with the deliverance of Israel from her tribulations and the commencement of the reign of the Lord of hosts. And if the resurrection of the Lord's people occurs at the beginning of the millennium, this, according to 1 Thess. 4:17, would also indicate the coincidence of the Rapture with end of the Tribulation and the beginning of the millennium.

Recognizing this difficulty for their timetable, pre-tribulationists have offered two solutions to the problem.

Some earlier proponents suggested that Isaiah does not describe bodily resurrection at all. Rather they suggest that the prophecy speaks of Israel's national restoration using symbolic language. Reese criticizes both Kelly and Gaebelein for this interpretation.

> If it is legitimate to spiritualize so clear a text as Isaiah xxvi. 19 on the resurrection of the dead, then those of us who insist upon the literal interpretation of the first resurrection in Rev. xx. 4, are placed in circumstances of peculiar difficulty when arguing with post-millennialists. ...if pre-tribs are at liberty to spiritualize the first resurrection in the O.T., then it is clearly the hollowest inconsistency to cavil at those who explain away that resurrection in the New.[26]

Although frequently criticized for his tone, Reese's analysis appears valid. This answer to the problem necessitates a glaring hermeneutical inconsistency for premillennialists. Also, ascribing these texts to national restoration seems to be an impossible solution exegetically, even if one would allow for the hermeneutical inconsistency, given the Apostle's prominent and specific use of the passages in his clear statements concerning bodily resurrection in 1 Corinthians 15.

Walvoord advances—if not introduces—another answer to the difficulty when he suggests the possibility of *two* first resurrections. He admits the hermeneutical dilemma of the earlier pre-tribulationists and points out a "*growing tendency* to review the question of whether the Old

---

[26]Reese, *Approaching,* 37.

Testament saints are, after all, raised at the same time as the church."[27] The key part of his argumentation rests upon the claim that OT saints are never described as being "in Christ," thus, Walvoord argues, Paul's phrase in 1 Thessalonians 4 that the dead in Christ shall rise first "seems to include only the church."[28] In doing this, Walvoord and the pre-tribulationists since his time, have inserted a key theological presupposition of Dispensationalism—the distinction of Israel and the church (as redefined by Darby)—into the discussion. According to the system, this distinction goes beyond the national and earthly realms and reaches into the spiritual and organic nature of believers from different time periods. [29] This does not flow from a natural exposition of the passages, as will appear below, it is rather the introduction of a theological presupposition—a theological presupposition that notably, and of necessity, removes the OT saints from being "in Christ." The implications could not be more significant. Here is but one of many occasions where Dispensationalism's effort to defend its eschatology corrupts its soteriology.

---

[27]Walvoord, *Question,* 153. Emphasis added.

[28]Walvoord, *Question,* 154.

[29] For a fuller analysis of the system see: Fuller; John H. Gerstner, *Wrongly Dividing the Word of Truth* (Brentwood, Tennessee: Woglemuth and Hyatt Publishers, 1991); Keith Mathison, *Dispensationalism: Rightly Dividing the People of God?* (Philipsburg, New Jersey: Presbyterian and Reformed, 1995); or Reginald C. Kimbro, *The Gospel According to Dispensationalism* (Toronto: Wittenburg Publications, 1995).

In one of the most celebrated and detailed defenses of the pre-tribulational version of prophecy, J. Dwight Pentecost takes this evolving line of argumentation to even greater lengths when he suggests that the first resurrection consists of four stages: 1) Christ the firstfruits; 2) the NT church at the pre-tribulational rapture; 3) tribulation saints; and 4) OT saints.[30] This takes note of the additional category of believers during the Tribulation created by Dispensationalism's distinctions. He curiously places the resurrection of both the "Tribulation saints" and OT saints together at the Second Advent but nonetheless lists them as *separate* stages. This obviously flows from the necessity to assign them to different categories of saved people based upon the distinctions of Dispensationalism. But another difficulty presents itself once these distinctions are allowed. Walvoord emphatically states that at the Second Advent no translation occurs.[31] He says this in the midst of an argument seeking to provide distinctions between the Second Advent and the Rapture, but he creates a problem in the process. It is one thing to place the resurrection of OT saints at the Second Advent and distinguish this from the resurrection and translation of NT church saints at a pre-tribulation Rapture, no matter how difficult this proves exegetically, but it is another thing to leave a whole category of people which their

---

[30] J. Dwight Pentecost, *Things to Come* (Grand Rapids: Zondervan Academie Books, 1964 reprint), 411.

[31] *Question*, 64.

system creates out of necessity (the so called "Tribulation saints") without a point at which they are translated and receive their glorified bodies. Answering this difficulty would require another duplication of an event, given that by definition such a translation would virtually depict a second Rapture. There must be a point when living Tribulation saints are translated and a time for this event. Pentecost's suggestions about the first resurrection meet this need, at least with reference to Tribulation saints that died during the Tribulation, that Walvoord apparently overlooks, but even Pentecost appears to leave the matter of living Tribulation saints unaddressed.[32] Opponents, however, will wonder if Pentecost's suggestion of multiple stages of the first resurrection is simply an attempt to hide the *uniqueness* of pre-tribulationism's demand for an additional resurrection for the NT church by finding still more resurrections.

One could think that Paul's treatment of the "orders" of resurrection in 1 Corinthians 15 might give credence to Pentecost's multiple stages of the first resurrection, but in Paul's discussion of the "orders" of 1 Corinthians 15: 23-24,

---

[32] Should they discuss this problem, pre-tribulationists may by default place this translation at the conclusion of the millennium based upon their suggestions about the population of the millennium considered below in chapter 6, but the discussion there will show this is inaccurate and unnecessary. The real problem on this topic is a problem for all premillennialists of where to place the translation/glorification of any who may be converted during the millennium. Will conversion include glorification during that time?

the two orders that are clear are that of Christ and that of believers—"Christ the firstfruits, afterward they that are Christ's at his coming." A possible but debatable third order is that of the rest of the dead.[33] While not impossible (and even attractive for a premillenial viewpoint) this would require understanding "the end" (vs. 24) as the last in the sequence and as representing the ungodly dead. This would interpret "*telos*" as something like "the end [of the resurrections]" or "the remainder [of the dead]" which would refer to the resurrection of the unrighteous (thus paralleling the separation of the resurrection of the righteous from the resurrection of the unrighteous as found in Revelation 20 and Daniel 12 and agreed upon by all premillennialists) but this would not refer to additional groupings of *believers* according to Pentecost's suggestion of stages of the "first resurrection" which includes believers only (Rev. 20). More recent pre-tribulationists, perhaps sensing the weight of their dilemma, have taken up this possibility in the "orders" of 1 Corinthians and suggested that non-Dispensationalists also multiply stages of the first resurrection. Couch declares: "Even some of the earlier Bible scholars who do not accept a dispensational rapture see two

---

[33] For a discussion of this possibility see John Brown, *The Resurrection of Life* (Minneapolis: Klock and Klock Reprint, 1978), 134-142. For comment on others who suggest this interpretation but without endorsing it see F. Godet's commentary *in loc.*

resurrections in 1 Corinthians 15:23-24."[34] Couch, however, misleads at this point, for again, the possible additional resurrection would be the *unrighteous*, not a division in the resurrections of the righteous in the "first resurrection" as the Dispensational suggestions demand. So even given the possibility of a third "order" no additional stages of the *first resurrection* appear, only "they that are Christ's at his coming" (vs. 23). Any third "order" would not be part of the first resurrection.

One might suggest that even Pentecost's multiplication of first resurrections becomes insufficient once the distinctions of Dispensationalism are accepted. His use of the general designation "OT saints" fails to take into account the pre-Abrahamic saints who cannot be subsumed within Israel. He has suggested the necessity of a fourth stage of the first resurrection when adding the "tribulation saints" which according to Dispensationalism cannot belong to Israel or to the NT church. He should, given this presupposition, recognize the same situation with reference to the pre-Abrahamic saints. They cannot belong to Israel or the NT church. Thus of seeming necessity Dispensationalism should posit at least five stages to the first resurrection, when allowing Christ's resurrection to remain in the list, indeed more if the Dispensational distinctions among pre-Abrahamic saints are recognized. NT church saints, on this

---

[34] Mal Couch, ed. *A Biblical Theology of the Church* (Grand Rapids: Kregel, 1999), 122.

scheme, have a different time of resurrection than saints from all other dispensations, even though those saints must all be resurrected simultaneously at the Second Advent though they stem from multiple dispensations.

The question arises, if there is no temporal distinction between the resurrections of these believers from differing dispensations (as Pentecost and Walvoord admit), why should the resurrection of NT church saints be any different? If the argument is presented, as addressed below in another context, that NT church saints are promised deliverance from the Tribulation, that would apply to those *living* at the onset of the 70th week but would have no relevance for those who were already dead at the beginning of the Tribulation and awaiting resurrection. They are already going to be absent from the earth for the 70th week. No resurrection is necessary for them to escape the tribulation yet their resurrection definitely coincides with the Rapture. The Dispensational answer to this difficulty would certainly follow that their presence, however, is demanded in heaven during the Tribulation for events that occur there then. This will be addressed below, but even given this point (which will not be granted) it would remain to be proven that their *bodily* presence is required. They are, according to 2 Corinthians 5:8, already present with the Lord.

But these extended reasonings are unnecessary. The suggestion of multiple (and unsubstantiated) first resurrections remains insufficient to overturn the post-tribulational argument from these passages no matter what distinctions Dispensationalists introduce. The Apostle in writing to the Corinthians clearly addressed members of the NT church, yet he links their resurrection with Israel's resurrection, not only without introducing an interval or distinction between them, but with a specific statement that the resurrection of the NT Corinthian believers will be in fulfillment of Isaiah's prophecy to Israel: "*then shall be brought to pass the saying*" (15:54). One is clearly the resurrection of NT church saints. The other is clearly Israel's. The Apostle places them together. The conclusion that the resurrection of NT church saints occurs at the end of the Tribulation and coincides with the Rapture seems inescapable.

Daniel's Vision of Israel's Deliverance

> *And many of them that sleep in the dust of the earth shall awake, some to everlasting life, and some to shame and everlasting contempt (Daniel 12:2)*

While the KJV translation of this text seems contrary to the premillennial tenet of the separation of the resurrection of the righteous dead from that of the unrighteous by the intervening 1000 years as found in Revelation 20, another translation, agreed upon by Jewish and Christian scholars alike is offered by Tregelles:

> *And many* ***from among*** *the sleepers of the dust of the earth shall awake;* ***these*** *shall be unto everlasting*

> *life; but* ***those*** *[i.e. the rest not awakened at this time] shall be unto shame and everlasting contempt.*[35]

To this pre- and post-tribulationists would agree regarding their common premillennial outlook. The context of this passage, however, like Isaiah, supplies a clear temporal marker in the previous verse. This resurrection of the righteous takes place at the time when Israel "shall be delivered" from a "time of trouble such as never was since there was a nation." This harmonizes exactly with Isaiah's prophecy regarding the end of the tribulation and the dawn of the millennium.

The pre-tribulational treatment of this passage follows the unsuccessful reasoning discussed above in the Dispensational distinctions introduced into Isaiah's prophecy. Pre-tribulationism holds that there must be at least two first resurrections and that the one for the church simply does not appear in this passage. Walvoord attempts to shift the burden of proof:

> The reason that posttribulationists attempt to throw the burden of proof for a pretribulational rapture on their opponents is that they themselves have no proof to the contrary. The fact that Old Testament saints and tribulational saints are resurrected after the tribulation…raises the question why neither the translation nor the resurrection of the church is

[35] S. P. Tregelles, *Remarks on the Prophetic Visions in the Book of Daniel* (London: Sovereign Grace Advent Testimony, reprint 1965), 162. Emphasis added.

> mentioned in this event. While silence is not explicit, it is nevertheless eloquent in this case. If posttribulationists had one positive Scripture on the time of the translation, it would save them much complicated argument.[36]

The force of his argument escapes the reader. If the passage does not mention separate and unique events for the church, how does that prove such events will occur? Walvoord has simply assumed the existence of a separate resurrection and Rapture of NT church saints without evidence. If he means that the resurrection mentioned in the NT passages is a different resurrection from the one described here in Daniel, as he must, he has begged the question and still has not answered the fact that the NT passages *do* link the Rapture with Isaiah's prophecy. Daniel clearly describes the same event as Isaiah, thus Daniel's temporal markers are still relevant in confirming the time of the event. Also, Walvoord's charge that post-tribulationists have entered into "complicated argument" is puzzling. Theological complexity certainly accompanies the Dispensational argument, while simplicity lies on the Historic Premillennial side. What Walvoord elsewhere calls *undeveloped* (as cited above in reference to the Historic Premillennialism of the early church) he here calls complicated. Any complexity in the post-tribulational treatments arises as these writers engage the evolving pre-tribulational arguments, not as they present

---

[36] Walvoord, *Question*, 155

their own case. Daniel confirms that the resurrection of the righteous occurs when Israel is delivered from the Tribulation.

Job's Declaration

While the post-tribulationists Reese and Ladd omit the passage, thus it is omitted in the rebuttals, Job's statement merits brief attention.

> *For I know that my redeemer liveth and that he shall stand at the latter day upon the earth; and that after my skin worms destroy this body, yet in my flesh shall I see God (19:25—26).*

Evangelicals have long seen here Job's faith in the resurrection. Job foresees a time when his Redeemer will stand upon the earth and he in his flesh will see God. While Job obviously does not offer the detailed account of the deliverance of the future nation from a time of Tribulation and the onset of the millennial kingdom as do the prophets, the notable consistency of the detail he does offer with the details of those accounts is striking. Job knew that his redeemer lived and that he would stand at the latter day upon the earth. At the Second Advent Christ is publically revealed and stands upon the earth. His servant Job knew that he would be resurrected and join his redeemer to share in the event.

New Testament Evidence

Other relevant portions from the New Testament appear in later discussions so only a few texts receive attention presently.

At the conclusion of Christ's explanation of the parable of the wheat and tares he states: "then shall the righteous shine forth as the sun in the kingdom of their Father" (Matthew 13:43). The context is clear. The harvest is the end of the world (13:39) when the children of the wicked one are gathered and carried away while the righteous are gathered and enter the kingdom. Christ paraphrases the context of Daniel's remarks from above (12:3) in his explanation of the parable. This once again indicates that the resurrection accompanies entrance into the kingdom as the prophetic timetable has illustrated.

A portion of Luke 14:14-15 reads:

> *For thou shalt be recompensed at the resurrection of the just. And when one of them that sat at meat with him heard these things, he said unto him, Blessed is he that shall eat bread in the kingdom of God.*

Alexander Reese draws attention to the fact that while this passage gives no explicit time reference in the Lord's own statement about the resurrection of the just, nonetheless the hearer's response to the Lord's statement, which Luke includes, illustrates "how unmistakably the resurrection of the holy dead in Israel was linked with the coming of the Messianic Kingdom."[37]

It remains to mention but one portion from Paul at present. The major division of Romans 9-11 becomes a focal point in premillennial interpretation. Characteristically in Romans, Paul anticipates a natural question in the minds of his readers following something he has already said. In this case, the anticipated question concerns National Israel. Will there be a future for them? A lengthy discussion ensues. Paul explains that the judicial "blindness" that the Lord has sent upon Israel does not prevent individual Jews from coming to faith in Christ (11:5) but it does highlight the distinguishing characteristic of the present age—the fact that God is calling out from among the Gentiles a people for his name. Having reviewed this gracious purpose for the Gentiles during these days of Israel's hardening, Paul returns to the question of Israel's future. If the days of Israel's *chastening* have proven beneficial to the Gentiles, how much better will be the days of Israel's restoration?

> *Now if the fall of them be the riches of the world, and the diminishing of them the riches of the Gentiles; how much more their fullness (11:12)?*
>
> *For if the casting away of them be the reconciling of the world, what shall the receiving of them be but* ***life from the dead*** *(11:15)?*

[37] Reese, *Approaching*, 59.

While some commentators wrestle with whether to take this "life from the dead" figuratively or literally, thus impacting one's millennial outlook,[38] the common premillennial and literal understanding of the passage views this as the resurrection. This provides another confirmation of the coincidence of the resurrection and the beginning of the kingdom. When Israel is received the resurrection occurs. When will Israel be received? That will occur when they finally turn in repentance and faith to the one they previously esteemed as "smitten of God and afflicted" (Isaiah 53) and yet whom they will at His gracious deliverance of the nation at the close of the Tribulation understand "was wounded for their transgressions."[39] The resurrection occurs when Israel inherits the kingdom. The scriptural timetable for the resurrection remains consistent.

Additionally S. P. Tregelles offers the telling observation from Paul's treatment of National Israel in Romans that this blindness prevails "*until* the fullness of the Gentiles be come in" (11:25). According to any pre-tribulational reckoning, the fullness of the Gentiles must reference the NT church in its completion. Tregelles, however, points out that on a pre-tribulational scheme this would mean that Israel's blindness is removed *prior* to her entering into covenant with

---

[38] John Murray, *The Epistle to the Romans*, Vol. 2 (Grand Rapids: Eerdmans, 1959), 84.

[39] For a wonderful exposition of Isaiah 53 as a future penitential psalm flowing from the heart of Israel, see David Baron, *The Servant of Jehovah* (Minneapolis: The James Family Publishers, 1978 reprint).

Antichrist, and seven years before her reception of Christ and her national restoration![40] Such a scenario seems impossible, but becomes necessary on a pre-tribulational understanding.

Conclusion

The link between the resurrection of the righteous and the Rapture of the church places an insurmountable difficulty before pre-tribulationism. An undisputed text describing the Rapture of the church (1 Thessalonians 4:17) locates the Rapture at the resurrection of the saints. Scripture repeatedly places that resurrection at the conclusion of the Tribulation when Israel is delivered and the millennial kingdom is established. The only vehicle open to pre-tribulationists is to introduce an additional first resurrection for NT church saints in distinction from the saints of all other dispensations. This sets in motion the necessity of recognizing a minimum of four "first resurrections," all of which occur at the same time except for the resurrection of the NT church which is claimed to precede the Tribulation. This rests solely upon an unsubstantiated theological presupposition of distinguishing the resurrection of Israel from the resurrection of NT church saints, and that presupposition proves demonstrably false given the specific identification of the resurrection of NT church saints in 1

---

[40] Tregelles, *Daniel,* 109-110.

Corinthians 15 with the resurrection prophesied for Israel at the end of the Tribulation described in Isaiah.

Chapter 4

IS THE RAPTURE IMMINENT?

Much of the remainder of this book supplies a critique of pre-tribulational arguments rather than a pairing of positive arguments from each side because both parties agree that Christ returns at the Second Advent. Post-tribulationists simply maintain that the Rapture occurs at this one undisputed coming. Although the final chapter will address such positive evidence for the Historic Premillennial view, it should seem hardly necessary seeing that the opponents of that viewpoint already agree that Christ does return at that time. It bears repeating that the burden of proof rests upon those who suggest the additional coming. If that fails, premillennialists of opposing persuasions really introduce a needless requirement when they ask post-tribulationists for further evidence to establish the fact of the Second Advent which they themselves already maintain. By the very nature of the case the real debate lies in the question of whether or not the arguments for the additional coming are convincing.

Although lists of arguments put forward to support pre-tribulationism often extend to great lengths,[41] serious evidence advanced to meet the burden of proof can be reduced to five general arguments. These arguments find repetition in a vast number of books and articles and provide the backbone of support for pre-tribulationism. This chapter and the next four chapters provide an analysis of these key arguments.

The first and potentially the most decisive argument in favor of pre-tribulationism and against all other views of the Rapture is the pre-tribulational doctrine of imminence. If no other predicted event must intervene or even *can* intervene before the church's translation occurs, obviously the Rapture is pre-tribulational. The prominence of this doctrine caused the titles "Any Moment Theory" and "Secret Rapture" to take root in the popular nomenclature surrounding emergent pre-tribulationism.

In his critique of pre-tribulationism, Robert Gundry, however, interestingly suggests that imminence need not demand pre-tribulationism, merely that it raises the possibility of pre-tribulationism on a "sliding scale" as

---

[41] Pentecost's list of proofs extends to 28 arguments, *Things*, 193-218. Walvoord exceeds this measure and marshals "Fifty Arguments for Pretribulationism" as his final chapter in *Question*. Repetition and logical fallacies are not difficult to discover in these lists. Some of these will appear below.

opposed to the post- and mid-tribulational positions.[42] But this focuses on a broad definition of imminence.

> By common consent imminence means that so far as we know no predicted event will *necessarily* precede the coming of Christ. The concept incorporates three essential elements: suddenness, unexpectedness or incalculability, and a possibility of occurring at any moment.[43]

He continues and states, "but these elements would require only that Christ *might* come before the tribulation, not that He must....it is singularly strange that the most popularly cherished argument for pretribulationism should offer such an obvious and critical limitation." Gundry argues here on technicalities. However, the usage among pre-tribulationists

---

[42] Robert H. Gundry, *The Church and the Tribulation* (Grand Rapids: Zondervan, 1973), 29.

[43] Gundry, 29. His reference to "common consent" is undocumented but may reflect some earlier opinion. Imminence usually occurs within pre-tribulational literature as demanding pre-tribulationism. See an interesting and perhaps unguarded exception in Chafer's statement:

> Whether it be that coming of Christ to the earth in glory when Israel is to be delivered or that coming into the air to receive His Bride, the coming is imminent. Scripture which directs Israel in the tribulation,... warns her to *watch*, for He will then come "as a thief in the night" (cf. Matt. 24:32-25:13; 1 Thess. 5:1-8; 2 Pet. 3:8, 10).

Lewis Sperry Chafer, *Systematic Theology, IV* (Dallas: Dallas Seminary Press, 1948), 367. This contrasts directly with most treatments of imminence and was altered in Walvoord's revision of one of Chafer's works. Lewis Sperry Chafer and John F. Walvoord, *Major Bible Themes* (Grand Rapids: Zondervan, 1974) 79-80.

and the prevailing understanding of the term in the overall eschatological debate indicate that it is necessary to draw a distinction between imminence and watchfulness in the case being made by pre-tribulationists, and in the remainder of the chapter Gundry ably makes this distinction which their view requires. Imminence in this environment carries the connotation that no other predicted event *can* precede the Rapture. Any investigation of the question must consider whether the calls for watchfulness which frequently appear in scripture actually require a doctrine of imminence in which no other prophetic event can intervene.

Before addressing the biblical evidence for imminence itself, it will be helpful to pause and note how some key intended *effects* of the doctrine of imminence appear in the pre-tribulational arguments. Gerald Stanton represents the common perspective when he states, "the purpose of such imminency is that the Church may be in a constant state of expectancy."[44] The beneficial effects that an imminent return would bring upon the expectant church viewed passively would include such things as encouragement and hope, and viewed actively as stimulating to holiness and service. Walvoord and most pre-tribulationists since his time have refined the focus to suggest that one of the specific aspects of comfort for the expectant church resides in her removal

---

[44] Gerald Stanton, *Kept From the Hour* (Grand Rapids: Zondervan, 1956), 109.

before the Tribulation begins.[45] Stanton vigorously continues the argument:

> By the very nature of the case, if the exact time of the rapture had been revealed, none but the final generation of Christians would have cause to look for the return of their Saviour, and for every other generation this vital hope and incentive would have been lost. Such is the mischief caused when any known event, such as the Tribulation, the coming of Antichrist, or the Millennium is thrust between the Church and the coming of Christ for His own.[46]

Stanton insists that in any scheme other than pre-tribulationism, only the last generation of Christians would possess a true expectation of Christ's coming and thus experience any of these beneficial effects. But post-tribulationists would counter by saying that nothing prevents every generation from assuming that theirs might be the generation in which the prophesied events transpire and the Lord returns. This criticism of the other perspectives leveled by the pre-tribulationists should rest instead only upon those who commit the error of setting a date, particularly a date where the predicted events would occur after their lifetime. Within a premillennial context, nothing except the setting of such a specific date would prevent every generation of Christians from assuming that the coming of Christ could

---

[45] Walvoord, *Question*, 80.

[46] Stanton, *Kept*, 109.

occur during their lives thus causing believers of every generation to live in expectancy.

One finds a telling argument against the pre-tribulational claim that only their outline of events can produce these motivational effects upon believers when he reads that the Apostle Peter urges just such an impact upon his readers when he addresses events which are clearly subsequent to the Tribulation.

> *But the day of the Lord will come as a thief in the night; in the which the heavens will pass away with a great noise, and the elements shall melt with fervent heat, the earth also and the works that are therein shall be burned up. Seeing then that all these things shall be dissolved, what manner of persons ought ye to be in all holy conversation and godliness, (2 Peter 3:10-11)*

Events held by all premillennialists *not* to be "imminent" are to have the same impact upon the life of the believer. Thus, the suggested effects which pre-tribulationists claim can only be produced by their doctrine of imminence cannot be weighed as evidence for pre-tribulationism. Scripture says that these effects should be produced in the lives of believers even when they contemplate events that they know will follow other recognizable events.

Moving on to the direct teaching of pre-tribulationists regarding imminence, in what some consider the *magnum opus* of pre-tribulational thought, J. Dwight Pentecost argues that while Israel receives signs for the approaching Second

Advent, the Church receives no signs for the Rapture. This imminence, he views as one of the key evidences for pre-tribulationism.[47] Amazingly his brief treatment of this key tenet includes only a parenthetical list of proof texts, which he leaves without comment. These texts include (John 14:2-3; Acts1:11; 1 Corinthians 15:51-52; Philippians 3:20; Colossians 3:4; 1 Thessalonians 1:10; 1 Timothy 6:14; James 5:8; 2 Peter 3:3-4).[48] In most cases the reader honestly struggles to understand why the text would be included as evidence for imminence. In cases where the reason is clear its validity must be challenged. For instance the Corinthians passage states that the translation will occur "in the twinkling of an eye," but this describes how quickly it will occur, not when it will occur. Nor does this passage imply that nothing else can occur before it happens. Also, as argued in the previous chapter, the whole context of 1 Corinthians 15 places the resurrection and the translation at the Second Advent. This text cannot establish imminence. Again, although not commenting on the Philippians passage, which states "for our conversation is in heaven; from whence also we look for the Saviour…," it appears that Pentecost's motive for including this as a proof text for imminence parallels his thought later on the same page where he states: "such passages as 1 Thessalonians 5:6; Titus 2:13; Revelation 3:3 all

[47] Pentecost, *Things*, 202-204.

[48] The reference cited is 1 Peter 3:3-4, but this is an obvious typographical error.

warn the believer to be watching for the Lord Himself, not for signs that would precede His coming."[49] In this he reflects the reasoning of Walvoord who boldly asserts that if believers are required to look for Christ this *precludes* them from looking for anything prior to Christ's appearing. This accounts for two of Walvoord's "Fifty Reasons" for pre-tribulationism and closely parallels a third.[50] But this must certainly be classed as *non-sequitur* reasoning. Looking for Christ, waiting for Christ, hoping and praying for his coming, do not in any way preclude the possibility or even the knowledge that other events must intervene before the coming one is watching for. Perhaps the strongest suggestion from these texts comes in Walvoord's claim that John 14 teaches that when Christ returns he takes believers to "the Father's house." This he insists must refer to heaven.[51] This does not argue imminence from the text but does provide comment based upon the supposed destination of believers after the Rapture as discussed earlier. But the text does not establish this. The earthly New Jerusalem could just as easily meet the description, and further, the passage provides no temporal indicators and certainly does not indicate an imminent coming.

---

[49] Pentecost, *Things*, 203.

[50] Walvoord, *Question*, 195-196, 198.

[51] Walvoord, *Question*, 75-78.

The remaining proof texts Pentecost offers appear below. The reader is asked to determine for himself if these passages demand or even suggest an imminent coming.

> *Which said also, Ye men of Galilee, why stand ye gazing up into heaven? This same Jesus, which is taken up from you into heaven, shall so come in like manner as ye have seen him go into heaven (Acts 1:11).*
>
> *When Christ, who is our life, shall appear, then shall ye also appear with him in glory (Colossians 3:4).*
>
> *And to wait for his Son from heaven, whom he raised from the dead, even Jesus, which delivered us from the wrath to come (1 Thess. 1:10).*
>
> *That thou keep this commandment without spot, unrebukeable, until the appearing of our Lord Jesus Christ (1 Timothy 6:14).*
>
> *Be ye also patient; stablish your hearts: for the coming of the Lord draweth nigh (James 5:8).*
>
> *Knowing this first, that there shall come in the last days scoffers, walking after their own lusts, and saying, Where is the promise of his coming? For since the fathers fell asleep, all things continue as they were from the beginning of the creation (2 Peter 3:3-4).*

Nothing in these passages demands or even suggests the pre-tribulational doctrine regarding imminence. Interestingly Pentecost and most other pre-tribulationists omit passages containing some of scripture's most likely references to imminence. These occur in the Olivet Discourse where the reader finds the following statements:

> *But of that day and hour knoweth no man, no, not the angels of heaven, but my Father only (Matthew 24:36).*
>
> *Watch therefore: for ye know not what hour your Lord doth come (vs. 42)*
>
> *Therefore be ye also ready: for in such an hour as ye think not the Son of man cometh (vs. 44).*

Eager to make use of these passages omitted by other pre-tribulationists, Allen Beechick builds a whole case for pre-tribulationism on the supposition that scripture posits two days, a *known* day and an *unknown* day—the known day being the Second Advent and the unknown day being the pre-tribulation Rapture. Taking the event of the abomination of desolation as the exact midpoint of the Tribulation, he suggests that those living during the Tribulation will be able to count out the 3 and ½ years as 1260 days (based on prophetic years of 360 days) and predict with precision the very day of Christ's return.[52] This brings the Second Advent into the category of a known day, so there must be another "unknown day" to which Christ refers in the Discourse. This makes room for the pre-tribulation Rapture. (He and others

[52] Allen Beechick, *The Pre-Tribulation Rapture* (Denver, Colorado: Accent Books, 1980), 8-38. Though published prior to Beechick, Gundry analyzes the possibility of such an approach in a section touching the "Predictability" of the Rapture (*Church,* 41-43).

do not consider the possibility that the Lord's statement of the unknown nature of the time of his return could simply mean that at the time he uttered the statement no one knew, and no one in the future would be able to set the date, but that there would come a time when his disciples would know that the day he then said was unknown would be *near*, just as the passage describes). But Beechik's "known day/unknown day" distinction raises several difficulties. Since the Olivet Discourse clearly references the Tribulation and speaks directly of a post-tribulational coming of Christ to gather the "elect" (vs. 29-31), most pre-tribulationists refuse to place the NT church in the Discourse at all, suggesting that it belongs exclusively to Israel. (Reese describes the treatment Kelly and Gaebelein give to the "Elect" in the Discourse as "their half-converted, half-Christian, Jewish Remnant").[53] Beechick, desirous to claim the language for pre-tribulationism, suggests the difficult solution of alternating back and forth within the Discourse between pre-tribulational applications and post-tribulational applications, even alternating which day is in view several times within successive verses.[54] He confesses his motivation:

> Because this statement occurs in a post-trib context, many pre-tribulationists felt they had to forfeit their strongest statement of imminence in the entire Bible. Relying on weaker verses to prove their case for imminence has not been very convincing to post-

---

[53]Reese, *Approaching,*208.

[54]Beechick, *Pre-Tribulation,* 262-263.

> tribulationists. Now, however, with the double reference interpretation, this strongest statement of imminency is rescued for pre-tribulationists to use once again.[55]

Even though Walvoord wrote an endorsement of the book as a convincing new contribution to the debate, few pre-tribulationists would follow Beechick in this particular endeavor, although Gundry criticizes Leon Wood for a similar approach and states, "a glance ...will show how violently such an interpretation wrests the section on watching from the section which treats the posttribulational advent."[56] Truly this represents textual manipulation or reading into the text in the extreme. Most Dispensationalists avoid the difficulty by simply refusing to find the church in the Olivet Discourse at all.[57] The difficulty here falls back on the Dispensational presupposition that must underlie this conclusion. The disciples were clearly the founders of the NT church. How were they, or the readers of the Gospels today, to know when they were to view themselves as representatives of National Israel or as representatives of the

---

[55]Beechick, *Pre-tribulation,* 268.

[56]Gundry, *Church,* 34.

[57] This has proved difficult for serious pre-tribulational advocates since many popular presentations of the doctrine have often given direct application of the language of the "thief in the night" to the Rapture when in context it is post-tribulational. Also the references to those taken away have been applied to believers who are taken in the Rapture when the ones taken away are those taken into judgment.

suggested new forthcoming distinct body of the NT church as Dispensationalism claims?

A further attempt to establish the doctrine of imminence appears in a form that has become common in the debates surrounding Dispensationalism. Opponents of Dispensationalism are accused of spiritualizing passages that should be interpreted literally. Volumes have been written by Dispensationalists since the mid-twentieth century making this charge against opponents of numerous persuasions. The Rapture debate has proven no different. Pentecost boldly states on page one of his treatise: "The basic differences between the premillennial and amillennial schools and between the pretribulation and posttribulation rapturists are hermeneutical, arising from the adoption of divergent and irreconcilable methods of interpretation." Then follow several pages of illustrations of this fact as it applies to the millennial debate, but no documentation appears with reference to the post-tribulational premillennialists he has accused of spiritualized interpretation in the same sentence! Walvoord also brings the hermeneutical charge directly to the post-tribulationists when he states:

> Other exhortations in relation to the return of Christ for the church also lose much of their meaning if the doctrine of imminency is destroyed. It should be obvious that only flagrant spiritualization of the

> tribulation passages…can possibly save the doctrine of imminency for the posttribulationist.[58]

In this charge of "spiritualization" Walvoord appears to imply that post-tribulationists must reduce the tribulation to an unrecognizable series of events in their endeavor to retain a doctrine of imminence. He leaves this charge undocumented. (He could perhaps, as Ryrie,[59] apply this criticism to J. Barton Payne's "imminent post-tribulationism", but this is invalid because Payne does not represent Historic Premillennialism nor its understanding that the 70th week of Daniel is still future). Walvoord also seems to assume that everyone would wish to maintain imminence as pre-tribulationism defines it, and that the post-tribulationists must surrender a fundamental point of interpretation in order to accomplish this desire. This misses the mark from yet another vantage point. Post-tribulationists simply do not believe the Bible teaches the imminence demanded by pre-tribulationism nor do they believe that fact to represent a weakness in their position.

One additional thought merits attention before leaving the discussion of imminence. In his chapter concerning the difference between expectancy and imminence, Gundry includes the observation that the disciples received instruction regarding matters that assumed a delay in the

---

[58] Walvoord, *Question*, 79.

[59] Charles Ryrie, *Dispensationalism Today* (Chicago: Moody Press, 1965), 91.

Lord's return. Peter was informed that he would die as an old man. The gospel was to be preached to all nations. These and other statements by the Lord implied some measure of delay in his return. Gundry concludes: "...if a delay in the Parousia of at least several years was compatible with expectancy in apostolic times, a delay for the several years of the tribulation is compatible with expectancy in current times."[60] While many may dismiss this as irrelevant—applying only to the first few decades of church history—one must however question whether the apostles could give instruction, now quoted as demanding imminence, to those for whom they knew such imminence did not apply.

The pre-tribulationists' use of scripture in the attempt to establish imminence proves unconvincing. The Historic Premillennial position maintains that scripture enjoins *watchfulness.* This watchfulness, however, does not demand or imply imminence in the way pre-tribulationists wish to apply the term. There remains an *ignorance* of the specific day and hour—but even this ignorance will wane as the day approaches and believers "will know that it is near, even at the doors"(Matthew 24:33). The Apostle Paul echoes this understanding when he writes that the ungodly will be caught unawares by the Lord's return, but that believers will not be in darkness that that day should overtake them as a thief (1 Thessalonians 5:4). Written to the Thessalonians,

---

[60] Gundry, *Church,* 37.

this passage does not offer room for the Dispensational argument that it must be applied to National Israel and not to the NT church. The scriptures simply do not teach imminence in the way that pre-tribulationism demands. Instead they teach watchfulness.

Chapter 5

IS THE CHURCH APPOINTED UNTO WRATH?

The second major argument to support the additional coming within pre-tribulationism appears in the claim that the NT church cannot be present during the Tribulation because God's wrath is poured out during the period and the church is promised exemption from God's wrath. Reiter observes that the success of Gundry's critique of pre-tribulationism stirred quick responses by pre-tribulationists who recognized the need for better scholarly defenses. [61] While not entirely absent from earlier discussions,[62] in this renewed effort by pre-tribulationists, a new prominence was given to the argument that the church is promised deliverance from wrath. This wrath came to be *defined* as the

[61]Reiter, "Development," 40-41.

[62] In fact, one might argue that this feature of pre-tribulationism was foundational during the initial Irving/Darby period.

Tribulation period. Though not usually presented in such terms, it will be helpful at the outset of this chapter to state this pre-tribulational argument syllogistically:[63]

> ***Major Premise***: NT church believers are promised deliverance from God's wrath.
>
> ***Minor Premise***: All people present during the Tribulation are subjects of God's wrath.
>
> ***Conclusion***: NT church believers cannot be present during the Tribulation.

This is not an attempt to misrepresent the argument and put the pre-tribulationists in a bad light. The facts of the case warrant the stark nature of this analysis. If, in order to come out from under God's wrath, the church must be removed from the earth before the Tribulation begins, both premises must be established. The argument rests upon this necessity.

Before considering the evidence, a point regarding mid-tribulationism should be interjected. The suggestion that the NT church will be present during part of the 70th week but removed for part, builds upon the assumption that this argument concerning removal from wrath is accurate. In fact, this part of the pre-tribulationists' case seems to provide the foundation of these other viewpoints. Rosenthal even chose to use this feature as the title for his new position, "*The*

---

[63] Though not stated in this form the elements of this syllogism are easily discerned in Reese, *Approaching*, 283. It really is an obvious description of the argument.

Pre-Wrath Rapture of the Church." Assuming this premise is correct, the question resolves down to what part of the week the wrath entails. Pre-tribulationists see it as entailing the whole of the week, mid-tribulationists view it as only the latter half of the week, and pre-wrath advocates only the last portion. If however this argument fails, that failure will weigh equally against all the mediating positions as it does against pre-tribulationism.

A closer analysis of the syllogism reveals the weighty demands of the conclusion. It must be NT church believers *alone* that receive deliverance from wrath. The fact that other believers are present on earth during the Tribulation without being removed (a fact admitted by pre-tribulationists) highlights this necessity. The uncomfortable but unavoidable consequence follows that according to this argument some believers are appointed unto wrath and some believers are not. This almost purgatorial corollary of the argument does not receive emphasis in pre-tribulational writings, for reasons which should appear obvious, but it is nonetheless a necessary consequence of this particular line of reasoning. The only alternative lies in suggesting that God provides some other measure of protection from his wrath (besides removal from the earth) for believers who are present during the Tribulation, but this removes the minor premise and the whole argument fails. The major premise demands that *only* NT church saints (as defined by Dispensationalism) are promised deliverance from God's wrath. It is not an unfair ploy or a distraction that frames the discussion in this way. The argument demands it.

Perhaps it will prove helpful to highlight an undercurrent at this point. Once again, the presuppositions of Dispensational theology arise in the Rapture discussion. Walvoord does not hide the fact that he understands pre-tribulationism to depend heavily upon Dispensational theology. While not found in the uncomfortable context of this discussion regarding wrath he nonetheless makes the following admission:

> All parties agree that there are saints in the tribulation and that even during this time of unprecedented trouble many will turn to Christ for salvation. If these believers in the tribulation are properly described as members of the church, it leads inevitably to the conclusion that the church will go through the tribulation.
>
> It is therefore not too much to say that the rapture question is determined more by ecclesiology than eschatology.[64]

He adds later:

> If the term *church* includes saints of all ages, then it is self-evident that the church will go through the tribulation...If, however, the term *church* applies only to a certain body of saints, namely, the saints of the present dispensation, then the possibility of the

---

[64] Walvoord, *Question*, 16.

> translation of the church before the tribulation is possible and even probable.[65]

Opponents would not argue with this assessment of the prominence Dispensational ecclesiology must receive in the debate (except in his conclusion that the distinction renders pre-tribulationism "probable"), and would even highlight the fact that this presupposition provides the foundation for pre-tribulationism. Ryrie agrees when he affirms:

> Pretribulationism has become part of dispensational eschatology. Originally this was due to the emphasis of the early writers and teachers on the imminency of the return of the Lord; more lately it has been connected with the dispensational conception of the distinctiveness of the Church.[66]

Gundry seems to be an exception to this norm. He suggests that there is no necessary connection between Dispensationalism and pre-tribulationism and even affirms that "posttribulationism accords well with a scripturally measured dispensationalism."[67] It appears, however, that Gundry's "scripturally measured dispensationalism" abandons the foundation of normative Dispensationalism—the dissociation of Israel and the NT church—in similar fashion to the subsequent movement of "Progressive

---

[65] Walvoord, *Question*, 19.

[66] Ryrie, *Dispensationalism*, 159-160.

[67] Gundry, *Church*, 28.

Dispensationalism".[68] Having acknowledged a measure of change within the NT era, he adds "the Scriptures also teach the essential unity of all saints. Dispensational distinctions between God's people are economical and transitory. At a deeper level all saints enjoy unity in Christ."[69] This lies at variance with the repeated assertions of recognized Dispensational spokesmen throughout the normative history of the system. Gundry later states, "We ought rather to recognize the *connection* of the Church with other dispensations and saints."[70] Statements such as these, bolstered by his scriptural argumentation, place him closer to Historic Premillennialism and its Covenantal orientation. Dispensationalists do not speak of the "connection" between the NT church and saints of other dispensations. The total

---

[68] See Darrell Bock, "Why I Am a Dispensationalist With a Small "d," *JETS*, September 1998), 383-396; Darrell J. Bock and Craig Blaising, *Progressive Dispensationalism* (Bridgepoint Books, 1993); Robert Saucy, *The Case for Progressive Dispensationalism* (Grand Rapids: Zondervan, 1993). The present writer believes those promoting the new category have abandoned Dispensational theology itself, retaining only premillennialism yet desiring to retain "Dispensationalism" in their title. Their *raison d'etre* lies in their acceptance of continuity between OT Israel and the NT Church. They take an 'already/not-yet' view of the kingdom. This should land them properly in the camp of Historic (non-Dispensational) Premillennialism. Their Dispensational critics largely comply with this analysis. See the 1995 revision of Ryrie's *Dispensationalism*, 161-181; also S. J. Nichols, "The Dispensational View of the Davidic Kingdom: A Response to Progressive Dispensationalism" *The Master's Seminary Journal* 7, (1996), 213-239.

[69] Gundry, *Church*, 21.

[70] Gundry, *Church*, 27, emphasis added.

dissociation of Israel and the NT church forms their bedrock premise. Thus it comes as no surprise when the normative Dispensationalist Paul Feinberg wishes to agree with Gundry regarding pre-tribulationism not being dependent on Dispensationalism (because this would obviously make the argument stronger), but must distance himself from Gundry at several points, notably his suggestion that saved Jews are part of the church during the Tribulation. For Feinberg this would bring difficulties, among which is the question, "Would each group preach a variation of the gospel, and so on?"[71] Feinburg obviously assumes this would be necessary because as a Dispensationalist he views the gospel preached in the church age as something distinct from God's dealings with National Israel. Mayhue echoes the same presupposition when he states "nowhere in Scripture is it taught that the church and Israel would coexist as the centers for God's redemptive message and yet remain mutually exclusive."[72]These writers seem to assume that post-tribulationists wish to operate with the mistaken Dispensational tenet that Israel and the church bring different, yet accurate, redemptive messages to the world. While seldom articulated explicitly, there seems to be an undercurrent among Dispensational writers that during the

---

[71] Paul D. Feinberg, "The Case for Pre-tribulationism" in *The Rapture: Pre-, Mid-, or Post-Tribulational?*(Grand Rapids: Zondervan Academie Books, 1984), 49.

[72] Mayhue, "Why," 244.

Tribulation, Israel's position and worship will be an *acceptable* reversion to an OT economy. Whereas non-Dispensationalists deny this assumption and insist that there is one redemptive message and that during the NT era *and* the Tribulation period National Israel remains in apostasy and lives at variance with that one gospel message. How can a Tribulational National Israel be right with God while in covenant with Antichrist, all the while still rejecting the true Christ as their promised Messiah?! The fact is that the NT church has embraced *Israel's* Messiah while Israel has for a season rejected him. One of the great purposes of the NT church age is to provoke Israel to jealousy by the ingathering of believers from among the Gentiles (Romans 9-11). Would it not be possible that this effect would only increase during the Tribulation?

Consistent Dispensationalists and the critics of Dispensationalism ultimately agree. Pre-tribulational support lies more in the realm of the theological than the exegetical. It depends heavily upon the presuppositions of Dispensationalism. While present throughout the debate over the Rapture, nowhere is this overarching reality more displayed than in the argument concerning wrath. Revisiting the demands of the syllogism then, either 1) some believers *can* undergo God's wrath, or 2) no believers are present during the Tribulation, or 3) it is possible for the NT church to be present during the Tribulation. Option two is admitted to be false by all sides of the debate since it is so clearly contradicted in scripture. Option three removes any support for pre-tribulationism. Option one exposes a significant soteriological difficulty for Dispensationalism, but it is nonetheless the only option open for pre-tribulationists so they silently embrace this solution.

Ultimately theological arguments, however legitimate, must rest upon layers of exposition. The task lies in determining what theological conclusions are truly demanded from the relevant passages, so attention must now turn to the scriptural evidence pre-tribulationists offer.

1 Thessalonians 1:10 and 5:9-10

> *...and to wait for his Son from heaven, whom he raised from the dead, even Jesus, which delivered us from the wrath to come.*
>
> *God hath not appointed us to wrath, but to obtain salvation by our Lord Jesus Christ, who died for us that whether we wake or sleep we should live together with him.*

The language of these texts has reached deeply into the pre-tribulational consciousness. The church is "not appointed unto wrath." This phrase surfaces almost immediately in discussions regarding the Rapture. But in order for these passages to provide support for pre-tribulationism (in addition to the remarkable demand that they apply only to NT church saints and not to any other believers), two things must be true. First, the wrath in view must be a wrath that God pours out during the Tribulation. Actually, to be precise, the wrath in view must be equated with the Tribulation as *a period of time in itself.* This will become apparent as the discussion progresses. Second, removal from the earth must be the vehicle through which deliverance from this wrath takes place.

In his defense of pre-tribulationism Feinberg illustrates that the wrath of God appears in scripture frequently. It has been poured out in the past, and it presently abides upon unbelievers. Quoting from Stahlin he further observes two future outpourings of divine wrath: during the tribulation and in the final judgment itself.[73] He continues, "While it is certainly true that Christians will not experience the final judgment of God (Rom. 2:5, 8; 3:5; 5:9), 1 Thessalonians 1:10 and 5:10 seem to be speaking of the Tribulation before the end." He offers three reasons for reaching this conclusion regarding 1:10. Firstly he states, "the general context of the Thessalonian epistles is the day of the Lord." Secondly he highlights that the reference is to a "coming wrath" and thus draws a connection between it and the Lord's "coming." Thirdly he states that this wrath "seems related" to that of 5:9 which is "eschatological." But none of these reasons demand his conclusion. First, the suggestion that the Thessalonian epistles provide the "general context" of the day of the Lord does not meet the *specific* demands of pre-tribulationism's

[73] Feinberg, "Case," 52-53.

argument about the reference to "wrath" in the verses in question, particularly if the day of the Lord does not commence until the Second Advent.[74] Second, even granting the strained verbal connection he suggests between the "coming wrath" and the Lord's "coming," this does not answer *which* coming is in view (assuming there are two future comings). If it is the Second Advent (which scripture frequently associates with wrath) then pre-tribulationism gains nothing by the reference. Third, the connection with 5:9, which Feinberg states is "more striking," still only places the references in an eschatological context. It does not supply an answer to the eschatological detail that is in question. Pursuing that detail one finds that the evidence leads toward the post-tribulational advent when Christ comes "in flaming fire taking vengeance on them which know not God" (2 Thess. 1:8). Further, a mere "eschatological context" could also have reference to the eternal wrath meted out in the judgment. Feinburg's arguments are overly general and gratuitous.

In 1 Thessalonians the two paragraphs that close chapter 4 and open chapter 5 clearly give eschatological instruction. In the first paragraph Paul addresses an issue upon which he wished to give further information. He did not want the Thessalonians to "be ignorant" concerning the state of believers who had died. The resurrection of these

---

[74] Pre-tribulationists need to include the Tribulation period within the day of the Lord. Most others understand it commences at the Advent.

believers and the translation of those living at the time of Christ's coming will occur together. In chapter 5, however, he reviews information which he is confident the Thessalonians already "knew perfectly." In doing so he borrows the figure of the "thief in the night" from the post-tribulational coming described in the Olivet Discourse. Far from providing evidence of a pre-tribulational departure of the church, this passage locates the Thessalonians alongside the ungodly at the close of the Tribulation. The difference between the godly and the ungodly is not one of location but of expectation. Just as in the Olivet Discourse, the ungodly will be caught by surprise at the Lord's coming, but the watching church is "not in darkness that that day should overtake [them] as a thief (5:4)." They will be expecting it. They will "know that it is near, even at the doors" (Matthew 24:33).The parallels could not be more obvious.

Gundry offers a telling analysis of these two verses in the Thessalonian epistles which refer to wrath.

> Neither of these verses states the method by which God will save believers from wrath. Therefore both offer inconclusive evidence either for prior removal or for protection in the midst of it. For that matter, neither of the verses places the wrath to come in Daniel's seventieth week. Perhaps Paul has in mind eternal wrath, or the wrath poured out right at the second coming—a view favored by the contextual discussion of the day of the Lord, which will begin not until the posttribulational advent…Even if the wrath should begin to arrive already within the seventieth week (an interpretation which the context

> does not support), the method of exemption could still be preservation on earth; ...[75]

This exposes perhaps the greatest weakness of the pre-tribulationists' assertions. There is no reason to give such a limited and specific definition to the word "wrath" as the theory demands. What natural reading of the passages would equate the word "wrath" with "presence on the earth during a specific period of time?" Even if for the sake of argument one grants the claim that these texts refer to the specific outpourings of wrath that occur during the Tribulation, they simply cannot provide the conclusion demanded by pre-tribulationism. They do not address how the church is protected. Devising the intricacies of pre-tribulational removal of a certain category of people from the earth from these passages requires a huge leap to say the least. That leap flows from a theological presupposition and not from exegesis.

Revelation 3:10

> *Because thou hast kept the word of my patience, I also will keep thee from the hour of temptation, which shall come upon all the world, to try them that dwell upon the earth.*

Perhaps the strongest support for this line of argumentation by the pre-tribulationists is claimed from this

[75] Gundry, *Church*, 54.

promise of Christ to the church of Philadelphia. Recognizing the insufficiency of the Thessalonian passages to establish removal from the earth, Feinberg suggests that this passage confirms that detail. He heads a lengthy section treating this text: "The Church Is Promised Exemption Not Only From Divine Wrath But Also From The Time Of Wrath." [76] This reflects the near universal usage of the passage among pre-tribulationists.

A preliminary observation is necessary before an analysis of the text. Within Dispensational interpretation there has been a suggestion that the seven churches of Revelation 2-3 represent seven stages of church history. While interesting parallels have been attempted (although perhaps reflecting a limited Western perspective), the parallels break down and many have trended away from this as a valid interpretation of the letters. Pentecost, however, favors this view, ironically, as a "spiritual application."[77] Ryrie also acknowledges the acceptability of the application.[78] Ice and Demy retain the idea and offer the common outline with rough dates suggested.[79] Normally the commendable Philadelphia church is supposed to represent the post-Reformation church up through the missionary

---

[76] Feinberg, "Case," 63.

[77] Pentecost, *Things*, 151.

[78] Charles Ryrie, *Revelation*, (Chicago: Moody Press, 1968), 21.

[79] Thomas Ice and Timothy Demy, *Prophecy Watch* (Eugene, Oregon: Harvest House Publishers, 1998), 47.

movements concluding around the year 1900.[80] This popular understanding of the letters to the seven churches does not merit attention in the present study merely because of the widespread acceptance of this opinion in years gone by, but rather because of the inconsistency manifested among pre-tribulationists who hold this view of the seven letters and yet still claim the statement made to Philadelphia in (3:10) as a proof text for pre-tribulationism. In such a case, these proponents do not answer the difficulty raised by their use of a text written to a church which, according to their reckoning, represents a period of time that has already ended, while still applying it to the last generation of the church's history and to an event that has yet to occur. Attempts to avoid this pitfall by extending the Philadelphian age all the way up to the Rapture would make the following Laodicean period remarkably shorter than the others and would also prove self defeating by unacceptably locating part of the NT church (that part represented by Laodicea) in the Tribulation.[81] Proponents usually maintain that the Laodicean church, rebuked for its lukewarmness, represents the contemporary church subsequent to the inroads of modernism.

Leaving this fading theory of the seven letters and pressing now into the text itself, the key issues that emerge in

---

[80] J. B. Smith *A Revelation of Jesus Christ* (Scottdale, Pennsylvania: Herald Press, 1961), 62.

[81] Stanton, however suggests this outline, *Kept,* 48.

the discussion are two: what is the "hour of testing," and how will the church be "kept from" it? Granting for the moment that the "hour" in view may well have reference to some aspect of the Tribulation period, the question of the manner of the church's being "kept from" it (*tereso ek*) has received remarkable scrutiny. A portion of Gundry's treatment follows.

> There is but one other place in Biblical Greek (LXX and NT) where *tereo* and *ek* occur together, John 17:15: "I do not ask Thee to take them out of the world, but to keep them from the evil one." The parallels between John 17:15 and Revelation 3:10 are very impressive. Both verses appear in Johannine literature. Both come from the lips of Jesus. A probability arises, therefore, of similar usage and meaning. In John 17:15 the words "take out of" (*ares...ek*) mean to *lift* or *raise up* and *remove*. The expression gives an exact description of what the rapture will be, a lifting up and removal. Yet it is this expression against which Jesus throws *tereo ek* in full contrast and opposition. How then can *tereo ek* refer to the rapture or to the results of the rapture when in its only other occurrence the phrase opposes an expression which would perfectly describe the rapture?[82]

The argument is compelling. Christ does not pray in John 17 that the church would be physically removed from the situation, but that it would be protected from the dangers of

[82] *Church*, 58-59. Gundry also exposes a misuse of documentation by pre-tribulationists Thiessen and Abbot when referencing A. T. Robertson, 56.

the world while the church is still present in the world. He specifically prays that the church would not be "taken out of" the world but rather that it would be "kept from" the evil. It is the *latter* terminology—"kept from" while still present—that finds parallel in Revelation 3:10 where pre-tribulationists demand the phrase must mean the very thing with which it is *contrasted* in John 17—"taken out of." Obviously feeling the weight of Gundry's argument and the need of the support pre-tribulationism seeks from this key text, Feinberg devotes 10 of the 40 total pages of his presentation of the pre-tribulational position (in a counterpoint volume) to the question of the usage of the Greek in Revelation 3:10. Relying heavily upon the argument of Townsend, he suggests that the phrase means "to keep outside of."[83] Douglas Moo, who critiques Feinberg in the same volume, rejects his conclusion. Notably, while allowing its possibility against the improbability of the other suggestions, Moo also diverges from Gundry's translation.

> Thus, we reject four different meanings commonly attached to the phrase *tereo ek*: "removal from" (Pentecost); "keeping outside of" (Townsend/Feinberg); "removal from the midst of"; and "Protection issuing in emergence" (Gundry). The first and third rest on an incorrect rendering of *tereo*; the second on an unestablished definition of *ek*; the fourth, while possible, does not do justice to the parallel texts. The rendering of the phrase suggested by our interpretation, "protection from" (with the

[83] Feinberg, "Case," 71.

> implication that the danger from which one is protected is present) best accounts for the lexical data and the sense the phrase has elsewhere in biblical Greek.[84]

This nuanced variation which Moo offers, however, still retains Gundry's conclusion. The church is present for whatever the trial is. It is just protected or brought through it. In his commentary on the passage Osborn concludes, "the view that sees this as protection rather than exemption from the trial is more likely."[85] Given these considerations, and especially the strong parallel in Christ's prayer for the church in the midst of the world in John 17, "*tereo ek*" falls far short of providing evidence for the strong demands pre-tribulationism places upon the passage.

The next matter of importance in this text concerns the meaning of the phrase "hour of temptation." Given the foregoing observations concerning the first phrase "kept from," the pre-tribulationalists' case fails even if the other necessity for their argument surrounding the phrase "hour of temptation" meets their criteria. While many consider it a settled matter that the reference is to the horrors of the Tribulation period as inflicted *by God* upon those dwelling upon the earth (hence the whole point of this argument

---

[84] Douglas J. Moo, et.al., *The Rapture: Pre-; Mid-; or Post-Tribulational?* (Grand Rapids: Zondervan Academie Books, 1984), Response to Feinberg, 97-98.

[85] Grant T. Osborn, *Revelation: Baker Exegetical Commentary on the New Testament* (Grand Rapids: Baker Academic, 2002), 193.

stemming from the church not being appointed to endure the wrath of God), the discussion often shifts imperceptibly onto the persecution inflicted *by Antichrist* upon believers. Feinberg, without noticing his shift on this point, muses "one might wonder in what sense they are 'preserved'"[86] as he challenges the post-tribulational expectation that believers will be present during the Tribulation. Such is the devastation Revelation describes as visited upon the martyrs of the Tribulation that Mayhue similarly remarks, "of what worth is the promise?"[87] But although a vast number of believers will perish during the Tribulation this still may not negate the promise of protection even if the protection in view were protection during persecution meted out by others and not wrath meted out by God. One might compare the comfort of Matthew 24 which says that "for the elect's sake those days will be shortened." This providential care for a remnant could be coextensive with the preservation promised. But this applies only if the protection in the text focuses upon a persecution imposed by the ungodly, and the pre-tribulational argument hinges upon the church being delivered from a wrath imposed by God. Pre-tribulationists gain nothing by arguing that the post-tribulational understanding of "protection within" must be in error

---

[86] Feinberg, "Case," 64. Stanton, however, rebukes post-tribulationists for missing the distinction between persecution inflicted by men and wrath poured out by God (34, 40, 42-43). His treatment still falls short of making the pre-tribulational case.

[87] Mayhue, "Why," 249.

because so many believers perish under the persecution of Antichrist. Their argument rests solely upon the supposition that the text refers to the wrath *of God*.

There is another perspective on this passage, however, that has not received sufficient attention. Focus should be drawn to a third phrase in the text. The text specifies that the hour of temptation comes upon "them that dwell upon the earth." These "earth dwellers" appear in the Revelation a total of eleven times. In this description "the enemies of the church are always in mind."[88] Even pre-tribulationists recognize this description and limit it to the ungodly.[89] It is a key literary device within the book. While Gundry does devote a brief paragraph to this observation,[90] both sides of the argument remain virtually silent on this point when discussing the hour of temptation and yet it could not be more relevant. If the "hour" will come *specifically* upon the ungodly (as delineated in the phrase) then one of two things must be true. It either comes upon the "earth dwellers" while believers are present but it only impacts the ungodly "earth dwellers," or it impacts these ungodly alone because no

---

[88] Robert H. Mounce *The Book of Revelation* (Grand Rapids: Eerdmans, 1977), 120. So Osborn, 193; and a large consensus of the commentaries. See also Thomas R. Schreiner, *New Testament Theology* (Grand Rapids: Baker Academic, 2008), 833. He calls it a "technical term for unbelievers."

[89] See Ice, *Prophecy,* 110, and his quotation from Robert L. Thomas, *Revelation 1-7: An Exegetical Commentary* (Chicago: Moody Press, 1992), 289.

[90] Gundry, *Church,* 60-61.

believers are present. All admit the presence of believers during the Tribulation, thus the "hour" clearly comes upon the "earth dwellers" while believers are present but exempt (or "kept from" it). In this one observation the pre-tribulational argument from the passage fails.

But another question follows. Is there evidence of a particular temptation or trial that will "come upon those that dwell upon the earth" in which they are distinguished from the godly alongside them? Two other key eschatological passages focus thought in this direction. In Matthew 24:24 Christ states:

> *For there shall arise false Christs, and false prophets, and shall show great signs and wonders; insomuch that, if it were possible, they shall deceive the very elect.*

In 2 Thessalonians 2:9-11 Paul seems to parallel this description of the deception that will prevail among unbelievers during the rise of Antichrist. Here, however, Paul adds to the "lying wonders" that Satan and the Antichrist will perform, the fact that in those days God will, upon those who receive not the love of the truth, send "strong delusion that they should believe a lie." Thus a twofold danger will present itself during the career of Antichrist. In addition to the deceptive wonders being wrought by the Man of Sin, a divinely outpoured delusion will afflict unbelievers during that hour.[91] Given these realities it is entirely possible that the "hour or testing" in Rev. 3:10 could refer to the temptation and choice incumbent upon men during the reign of Antichrist. Will they believe "*the* lie" (the article is present in vs. 11) and follow Antichrist, or will they reject him and follow the true Christ? While it is not necessary to define the "hour of temptation" with such precision in order to settle the questions concerning the Rapture debate from Revelation 3:10, this suggestion merits consideration.

This passage cannot rise to meet the burden of proof placed upon it to support an additional coming of Christ. The weight is too great and the argument too dependent upon improbable usages within the language. Even Walvoord senses the insufficiency of this passage to support such weight when he weakly concludes, "While it may be debatable to what extent this constitutes absolute proof for pretribulationism, it gives no comfort whatever to posttribulationism."[92] Post-tribulationism does not need comfort. Pre-tribulationism needs evidence. Though many pre-tribulationists place exceedingly heavy reliance upon this text, it simply cannot bear that burden.

---

[91] Stott makes the astute observation that the passage does not highlight a lack of knowledge of the truth, but a lack of love for it. John R. W. Stott, *The Message of 1 & 2 Thessalonians* (Downers Grove, Illinois: Intervarsity Press, 1991), 172-173.

[92] Walvoord, *Question*, 70-71.

2 Peter 2:9 and Typology

> *The Lord knoweth how to deliver the godly out of temptations and to reserve the unjust unto the day of judgment to be punished.*

Walvoord adds this to his list of proof texts for the NT church's removal in addition to the previous passages. Here he appeals to examples of typology. From this passage, using the example of Lot's deliverance before the destruction of Sodom he argues:

> While illustrations cannot properly be taken as proof, they confirm the idea that God characteristically delivers believers from wrath designed for judgment upon the unbelievers. If God delivers the church before the time of tribulation, it will be in keeping with this general principle.[93]

Ice and Demy also include typology as a secondary support for pretribulationism and suggest Enoch, Noah, Lot, and Rahab, as examples of God's delivering his people from times of wrath.[94] But arguments from typology, without direct indication of their meaning in scripture itself, must be held at arm's length. Lot may look attractive as a type who was removed from Sodom before its destruction, but post-tribulationists could suggest Israel as a type that was left in Egypt and yet was protected while God poured out the plagues. Elijah was not removed from the drought, but

---

[93] Walvoord, *Question,* 71.

[94] Ice, *Prophecy,* 112.

supplied with what he needed during the drought. The typology sword cuts both ways.

Additional Arguments Related to Wrath

Beyond suggesting these texts to support the argument, theological arguments by pre-tribulationists occur that should be considered sub-points of this major heading.

Often Dispensationalists demand that the church must be absent during the Tribulation based upon the supposed *purposes* of the period. Headings such as "The nature of the Tribulation" frequently occur in lists of evidence for pre-tribulationism. This line of argumentation appears in Walvoord, Pentecost, Chafer, and Ryrie as well as lesser known pre-tribulationists.[95] In such cases the suggestion follows that because of renewed focus and activity within National Israel the NT church cannot be present. The fact that the same situation existed in the days between the Ascension and the destruction of the Temple, escapes mention. The normal explanation offered is that after the church age ends with the Rapture, things resort back to an OT economy for the Tribulation period. But this again leaves pre-tribulationists open to the serious charge that they maintain Israel's worship during the Tribulation is acceptable after the church's message of the gospel has

---

[95] Walvoord, *Question*, 61-69; Pentecost, *Things*, 194f, 233f; Chafer *Systematic IV*, 364; Ryrie, *Basis* , 139f.

ended. According to the demands of Dispensationalism, whatever message is proclaimed during the Tribulation (a message Revelation 14:6 describes as the "everlasting gospel") the saints who receive it cannot belong to the church (but nor will they belong to National Israel). Pre-tribulationists frequently remind us that the Tribulation is the "time of *Jacob's* trouble" (Jeremiah 30:7, emphasis added). God deals with and chastens Israel during this period. The fact that these purposes for Israel unfold during the Tribulation, according to the theory, requires that the church be removed previously. The presupposition behind these suggestions accounts for several more of Walvoord's "Fifty Reasons." But none of this (as dangerous as it is to put forward, even if it were true) suggests that the church must be removed. This simply advances another *non sequitur* and involves the "purgatorial difficulty" regarding Tribulation saints mentioned earlier as well as the problems in soteriology mentioned here. How can these saints "from every tribe and kindred" be present during these events, while the "church" proper, according to the demands of the theory, cannot be present? Climactic events occurring within and upon the Nation of Israel during the Tribulation simply do not require the absence of the NT church.

Pre-tribulationists also frequently point out that the word "church" does not appear in Revelation chapters 4-19 (chapters chronicling the Tribulation) while it does appear in chapters 2-3. This is offered as indication of the church being absent. Thiessen is representative of a vast number when he states: "This is worthy of note because of its frequent occurrence in the first chapters and its appearance again in 22:16. If the church were on the earth, we would expect it to be mentioned frequently."[96] Two observations eliminate the force of this argument. First, it relies entirely upon the unsubstantiated presupposition that the tribulation saints that do frequently appear in these chapters are not part of the church. Would pre-tribulationists be amenable to the suggestion that because the word "church" does not appear in the salutation to the book of Romans that its recipients were not part of the church? That would carry as much weight as their claim from Revelation. There is no warrant for excluding the international believers identified in Revelation 4-19 from the church except for a preconceived theological requirement that they cannot belong to the church. Second, focusing upon the vocabulary proves nothing because the instances where the words "church" or "churches" do appear occur only with reference to the seven specific churches and the wording of the letters to them. This also accounts for the reference in 22:16.

The argument that the church must be removed before the Tribulation because it is "not appointed unto wrath" fails. The pre-tribulational exposition of the suggested passages is highly strained and unsuccessful. Scripture

---

[96] Henry Clarence Thiessen, revised by Vernon Doerksen, *Lectures in Systematic Theology* (Grand Rapids: Eerdmans, 1979), 378.

nowhere demands the premise which is necessary for the theory that all people living during the Tribulation are under the wrath of God, nor can it be established that the period itself should be identified as the wrath of God. The accompanying theological arguments also fail from a logical standpoint and introduce unnecessary and dangerous soteriological difficulties.

Chapter 6

IS AN INTERVAL NECESSARY?

Following the arguments regarding imminence and wrath, the evidence for pre-tribulationism begins to change in nature. The previous arguments held the potential of being exegetical. But as the previous chapters demonstrated, the exegesis of the passages put forward by pre-tribulationists has proven faulty. Usually those exegetical arguments necessitated an accompanying theological presupposition in order to make the argument work. The remaining arguments for pre-tribulationism lean almost exclusively upon theological considerations. Let it be clearly stated at this point, however, that theological argumentation is valid and at times forms a vital part of the church's work. History and reason show the validity of formulating doctrines from "good and necessary consequences"[97] of scripture. But the crucial factor in admitting theological

[97] *Westminster Confession of Faith*, I, vi.

argumentation is the *necessity* of the conclusions. That test must be applied to the remaining evidence for an additional coming of Christ.

The next major category of argument flows from the suggestion that certain events must transpire after the Rapture but before the Advent. While the scriptures surrounding these events do not themselves indicate a pre-tribulation Rapture, the claim of the necessity of an interval during which these events must occur is offered as support for pre-tribulationism. Actually, to be more precise, rather than providing evidence for pre-tribulationism, this line of argumentation presents itself as *disallowing* post-tribulationism since post-tribulationism obviously supplies no interval between the Rapture and the Advent. If there is need for such an interval for some events to occur, then of necessity post-tribulationism fails. This understanding of a category of argumentation brings several arguments together in this chapter which often appear separately.

The Judgment Seat of Christ

Pre-tribulational teaching surrounding the judgment of believers involves an assumption that believers are judged separately and at a different time from unbelievers. Thus the "Judgment Seat of Christ" (2 Corinthians 5:10) and the "Great White Throne" (Revelation 20) are sharply distinguished within pre-tribulationism.[98] Chafer serves as a classical spokesman when he states, "at the judgment of the great white throne there is but one class—the wicked dead."[99] However, one might pause before reading this large and important conclusion into the text. Revelation 20:15 may indicate by implication that the righteous are also present when it states: "And whosoever was not found written in the book of life was cast into the lake of fire." One might then assume that those who *were* found written in the book were present as well. A universal flavor presents itself in the way the judgment is introduced: "And I saw the dead, small and great, stand before God; and the books were opened…" (vs. 12). Chafer passes over this possibility saying: "The book of life is also in evidence, but probably with a view to demonstrating that no errors have been made and that those gathered before the great white throne have not the gift of God which is eternal life."[100] This seems a rather smug dismissal of a serious question.

Leaving the larger discussion of a General Judgment aside (where some disagreement among premillennialists of various persuasions on the Rapture may occur), in seeking support from the timing and the participants of the "Judgment Seat of Christ," the demands of pre-

---

[98] Unlike the separation of the resurrections, premillennialists do not universally maintain separate judgments. See Gundry, 163-164.

[99] Chafer, *Systematic IV*, 412.

[100] Chafer, *Systematic IV*, 411-412.

tribulationism are specific. Not only does pre-tribulationism require that this judgment include only believers, but the theory goes further and insists that the judgment only include NT church believers and that it must occur in heaven during the Tribulation. But the key passage, 2 Corinthians 5:10, supplies no specific time reference for the judgment. The context, however, does give some indication regarding the timing when it speaks of the "groaning" of the believer as he desires to be "clothed upon" with the glorified body that his "mortality might be swallowed up of life"(vs. 4). Hence the *resurrection* supplies the only temporal marker in the passage. Granted, this does not prove self-contradictory since within their own system the pre-tribulationists place the resurrection of NT church believers before the Tribulation, but given the discoveries outlined previously in chapter 3 concerning the time of the resurrection of the righteous dead, this passage does not locate the judgment of believers in heaven during the Tribulation. Rather every indication in scripture places this event at the Advent, thus, according to the context, the Judgment Seat of Christ must follow the Second Advent. This passage does not establish a pre-Advent timeframe, heaven as the location, nor a separate judgment for believers, all of which pre-tribulationism demands. These assumptions are simply gratuitous.

Similar to the pre-tribulationist's need for multiple "first resurrections" discussed in chapter 3, this argument clearly introduces the need for multiple judgments. One must realize at this point that this placement of the Judgment Seat of Christ in heaven following a pre-tribulation Rapture does not merely demand a separate judgment for believers in distinction from unbelievers (as other non-pretribulational premillennialists who argue against a General Judgment might also maintain), this involves the recognition of several distinct judgments including different groups of *believers* once the Dispensational presuppositions come into play. Gundry outlines the common pre-tribulational teaching of the judgments as follows:

1. The judgment seat of Christ for church saints
2. The judgment of the nations before the millennium
3. The judgment of living Israel before the millennium
4. The judgment of the wicked dead after the millennium.[101]

However, as before, one finds that even these distinctions do not finish the task once undertaken. Pre-tribulationists recognize and publish these distinct judgments, but they are not as forthcoming with recognizing the other judgments which become necessary once this time frame for the judgment of NT church saints is established. This outline omits the obvious question of the judgment of OT believers since they are not included in the pre-tribulation Rapture. When does their judgment occur? Pentecost fails to include

[101] Gundry, *Church*, 164.

this in his list of additional judgments.[102] Gundry expands even this question and observes a total of four additional groups he classifies as "loose ends"[103] unaccounted for by the pre-tribulational reckoning: 1) OT saints, 2) tribulation martyrs "who cannot be included by pretribulationists in the judgment of the living nations because the martyrs will have left their natural bodies through death," 3) those saved during the millennium, and 4) the wicked still *living* at the close of the millennium. This brings the total of "groups" needing their own time of judgment to eight once the pre-tribulational claim regarding the Judgment Seat of Christ is accepted! Actually, even this total would need expansion because it includes OT saints as a single category. Once the Dispensational distinction between OT Israel and the Pre-Abrahamic dispensations is recognized, one or more judgments would still need to be added. Recognizing these unintended problems for the pre-tribulational outline, Gundry muses:

> We may also observe that those who maintain the necessity of an interval between two phases of the Parousia in order to provide time for the judgment of Christians and the marriage supper of the Lamb themselves have crowded together four judgments—that of martyred tribulational saints, that of OT saints, that of the living nation of Israel, and that of living nations—between the posttribulational advent and the millennium. What has become of the

[102] Pentecost, *Things,* 412-424.

[103] Gundry, *Church,* 164-165.

> necessity for an interval in the pretribulational outline of events?[104]

This is a telling criticism. If a theological presupposition, which is used to frame an argument based upon the supposed necessity of an interval for the judgment of a particular group of people before the Second Advent, requires that additional groupings of people, created by the presupposition, be judged at the very time which the theory says it is impossible for the group in question to be judged, then the whole argument falls under its own weight. Rather than supplying evidence for the doctrine, the attempt to find support for pre-tribulationism based upon the Judgment Seat of Christ creates more problems than it solves. Solving those problems removes the very support the invention of the argument sought to create.

Walvoord, however, persistently advances another thought under this heading. He states, "The character of this judgment seems to set it apart from judgments occurring at the second advent. The rewards anticipated in this judgment are described as *imminent* in several Scriptures."[105] He is of course claiming that any implication that the judgment of believers is imminent (a doctrine already found to be lacking any support) implies that it cannot be associated with the Second Advent. His suggestion of 1 Peter 5:4 as evidence for this conclusion seems most precarious. Peter mentions the

---

[104] Gundry, *Church,* 165.

[105]Walvoord, *Question*, 90. Emphasis added.

reception of a *crown* of glory "when the Chief Shepherd shall appear." One might grant that the reception of crowns implies that judgment occurs at the event in view in the passage. But this text only establishes the "imminence" of the judgment if the appearing at which the crown is conferred is *itself* imminent. Walvoord reasons in a circle. He attempts to support pre-tribulationism on the assertion that the Judgment Seat of Christ is imminent, thus it must precede the Second Advent. He rests his claim of the imminence of the judgment upon the supposedly pre-established fact of the imminence of the appearing at which the judgment occurs, which is the very point he is seeking to prove! The same circular reasoning applies to his use of Revelation 22:12 as an additional proof text for this assertion regarding imminence: "And behold I come quickly; and my reward is with me." Nothing in the text supports his argument.

Pre-tribulationists also seek support for the early timing of the judgment from John's vision of the 24 elders in Revelation who have already received their crowns when they are mentioned. The common argument includes the following assumptions: 1) that they represent only the NT church; 2) that the chronology places them in heaven during the Tribulation; 3) their crowns indicate that the judgment has already occurred.[106] Ryrie observes a contrary interpretation that OT saints are also represented among the

[106] Smith, *Revelation,* 102-116.

elders but dismisses it as improbable since they do not receive resurrection until the Second Advent. He then curiously adds an apparent self-contradiction: "By either interpretation the church is included and is thus in heaven before the tribulation begins."[107] But if he allows one interpretation to include within the imagery those who are not in heaven during the Tribulation (only reckoning it improbable), why does he demand that others included in the imagery *must* be in heaven during the Tribulation? No matter what identity belongs to the elders, the assumptions of pre-tribulationism are open to serious objections. [108] Also, though probable, it is not conclusive that the elders represent the church. They could be celestial beings as found under a variety of figures in other prophetic scriptures. If they do represent the church, does that fact require that the *whole* church be present in heaven during the Tribulation? Could they not represent only members of the body of Christ who have gone before? Must they represent *only* the NT church as the theory requires? The use of the number 24, which occurs later in Revelation where the names of the twelve tribes and of the twelve apostles are written on the gates and foundation stones of the New Jerusalem, encourages the thought that they represent the saints of all ages. And if Israel

---

[107] Ryrie, *Revelation*, 36.

[108] The remainder of this paragraph summarizes Gundry, *Church,* 70-74.

is included in the figure then the vision cannot imply a pre-tribulation Rapture.

After noting McClain's boast of earlier scholars who did see the church (although without the Dispensational definition) in the vision of the elders, Gundry opines:

> But it is passing strange that a pretribulational rapture suggested itself to none of the thirty commentators cited, who did not approach the matter with the preconception that something in the passage ought to portray the rapture....If not a single one of these erudite scholars suggested, much less held to, a pretribulational rapture despite their opinion that the twenty-four elders represent the Church, we might reflect long before drawing a pretribulational conclusion ourselves.

None of the passages referencing the judgment of believers require that this judgment occurs in heaven while the Tribulation transpires upon the earth. Further, none of them clearly establishes a separate judgment for believers from unbelievers. That some do associate judgment or rewards with the coming of Christ proves nothing in the quest for evidence of an additional pre-tribulational coming. Judgment occurring at the Second Advent fits exactly within Historic Premillennialism.

The Marriage Supper of the Lamb

As discovered in the previous discussion, many pre-tribulationists also seek support for the necessity of an interval between the Rapture and the Advent by suggesting that the Marriage Supper of the Lamb must also occur in heaven while the Tribulation transpires upon earth. But this assertion creates its own difficulties and pre-tribulationists are not united on how to view the marriage or the bride.

In his argument for the pre-tribulational position Stanton remarks: "Without doubt, the whole wonderful scene takes place in heaven. The saints have all been raptured (for there will be *no partial bride*!), but as yet the revelation has not taken place."[109] This involves the difficult but frequent Dispensational assertion that the "bride" contains only NT church saints. If only those converted between Pentecost and the pre-tribulation Rapture constitute the bride, what is the relationship of other believers to Christ?

Many suggest with Stanton that the marriage supper must take place in heaven during the Tribulation.[110] However, Revelation 19 (which supplies the fullest reference to the event) seems repeatedly to place that event alongside events which are post-tribulational. The chapter opens with the phrase "After these things" which follows on from the destruction of the Beast and Babylon the Great described in the previous chapters. Also in vs. 6-7 the marriage clearly links with the *reign* of Christ as it reads:

---

[109] Stanton, *Kept,* 261. Emphasis added.

[110] Chafer, *Systematic,* 377; Pentecost, *Things,* 226; Walvoord, *Question*, 91; etc.

> *For the Lord God omnipotent reigneth. Let us be glad and rejoice, and give honor to him: for the marriage of the Lamb is come, and his wife hath made herself ready.*

The millennial reign begins at the close of the Tribulation after the victory over the Beast. The marriage coincides with these events. These events are all post-tribulational.

Sensing the difficulty, Thomas Ice has proposed that one must distinguish two events: the *marriage* and the *supper*. He suggests that the marriage must take place prior to the supper. But note that Ice does not merely suggest the priority of the marriage to the supper, he demands the *separation* of these events. One occurs in heaven, the other upon the earth. His sequence locates the Judgment Seat of Christ in heaven (where the worthiness of the bride is proved), then the marriage—still in heaven—occurring after the judgment but prior to the Advent, and finally the supper following the Advent on earth at the commencement of the millennium.[111] The context, however, militates against Ice's creative suggestion. Revelation 19 speaks of the "marriage supper" in vs. 9 but only the "marriage" in vs. 7. No distinction is suggested between them but rather they are used interchangeably in the text and appear to be synonymous. Further, and more telling for Ice's suggestion,

[111] Thomas Ice, "The Marriage Supper of the Lamb," http://www.pre-trib.org/data/pdf/Ice-TheMarrigeSupperoft.pdf (Accessed September, 2011).

one finds in vs. 7 where *only* the "marriage" is mentioned (if it were possible to distinguish the events), that this follows the defeat of the Antichrist and the establishment of the "reign." Ice's view would require that it be the supper, not the marriage that occurs then. This view not only requires reading into the text but doing violence to the text.

Attention should now return to the pre-tribulational requirement that the "bride" is made up of only NT believers and must *exclude* OT saints (of all dispensations), Israel, and the so called Tribulation saints. Israel is frequently spoken of in the OT as the wife of Jehovah. The imagery seems to illustrate continuity between Israel and the NT church rather than the dissociation demanded by Dispensationalism. The well known pre-tribulationist Donald G. Barnhouse offers an interesting solution for this problem introduced in the Dispensational theory by suggesting that there are two marriages, and two suppers that must be distinguished. His treatment of Revelation 19 includes a lengthy quotation from another unnamed commentator in which he argues that the answer to the difficulty (peculiar to Dispensationalists) of reconciling the figure of Israel as the bride of Jehovah and the NT church as the bride of Christ—without allowing either to be a part of the bride constituted by the other—is to view them as separate brides.

> The thought of a double marriage, …need not confuse us. In this event, the company that

> constitutes the bride of the one marriage would constitute the guests at the other.[112]

Having concluded that this distinction allows that "all the passages on this subject will be understood without difficulty," he forgets to inform the reader which wedding is in view in Revelation 19! He also adds that his unnamed commentator "cannot be positive of the identity of the company that here constitutes the bride." If it is the church, then Barnhouse's suggestion offers no support to pre-tribulationism since the marriage is post-tribulational.[113] If Israel's marriage supper is what Revelation 19 describes, as Barnhouse's unnamed source may hint, then no evidence, scripture passages, or time frame for the additional pre-Advent marriage supper for the church are offered, and if, as required by the theory, the church's marriage does occur previously, no explanation is given as to how an as yet unconverted and incomplete Israel can serve as the guests at that wedding. This ever increasing complexity of argumentation in an attempt to provide evidence for a pre-tribulation Rapture begins to weary the student when the simplicity of the Historic Premillennial vantage point creates no such problems of theology or exegesis to overcome.

---

[112] Donald Gray Barnhouse, *Revelation* (Grand Rapids: Zondervan, 1971), 353.

[113] He does not claim support for this particular argument in the context.

These suggestions including different marriages, distinctions between the marriage and the supper, different brides, and the varied sequences of events, etc., however, all fail once the identification of the bride comes under consideration. Inquirers must return to the fundamental question of whether or not it is possible to limit the identification of the bride (or one of the brides) to the NT church. John MacArthur, a more sober exegete on this point, recognizes that all saints must ultimately belong under this one description. He keeps to the normal Dispensational definitions to begin, but deviates as he develops his comment on Revelation 19:7.

> While the term "bride" often refers to the church, and does so here…it ultimately expands to include all the redeemed of all ages, which becomes clear in the remainder of the book.[114]

As MacArthur doubtless recognizes, the suggestions of limiting the bride to the NT church or of adding a second bride representing Israel are surely contradicted by the description of the bride that appears in Revelation 21:9. "Come hither and I will show thee the bride, the Lamb's wife." The verses that follow reveal the bride under the descriptive imagery of the New Jerusalem with the details added that the city has twelve gates which bear the names of the tribes of Israel, and twelve foundation stones which bear

---

[114] John MacArthur, *The MacArthur Study Bible* (Nashville, Tennessee: Word Publishing, 1997), 2019.

the names of the apostles of the Lamb. Clearer imagery establishing the essential unity of believers from both testaments is difficult to imagine, yet pre-tribulationism seeks support for itself by unnaturally dividing this unified body and demanding that one portion of it be judged, rewarded, and married in heaven in distinction from the *same* events which must transpire for another portion of the same bride at the Second Advent.[115]

While MacArthur has ultimately recognized the correct identity of the bride, his full treatment of the Marriage Supper, however, fails under scrutiny. Conflict arises between his theological fidelity to pre-tribulationism and his exegetical fidelity to the text. He follows a common pre-tribulational argument when he compares three stages in a Jewish wedding to events between Christ and the NT church: (1) Betrothal: which he defines as election in eternity past; (2) Presentation: which he defines as the church being presented to Christ at the pre-tribulation Rapture; and (3) Ceremony: which he argues will conclude with the Supper described in Revelation 19. He fails to answer his inconsistency in limiting stage 2 to the NT church while ultimately including all saints of all ages in stage 3 in his exposition of the bride. And although he does not illustrate his own inconsistency in his treatment of the first stage as he

---

[115] That is unless one accepts the classical Dispensational view that Israel is never part of the Bride and only an observer. This raises soteriological difficulties again, and contradicts the description of the city.

does in the third, does this mean that MacArthur only includes NT church saints in the eternal election of individuals to Christ in stage 1? This seems impossible. So, one is left with the inevitable understanding that in the Betrothal/Election (stage 1) and the Ceremony/Marriage (stage 3), all saints of all ages are included, but that in the Presentation/Rapture (stage 2) only NT church saints are included.

It is all too strained and unconvincing. Straightforward reading of the relevant passages would not lead to these conclusions if the idea of a pre-tribulation Rapture were not previously established in one's mind. Once established, such an idea, even in seeking support for itself, yet again creates more problems than it solves when it seeks to explain the Marriage Supper of the Lamb.

The Population of the Millennium

The final issue raised under the claim of the necessity of an interval between the Rapture and the Advent displays an even more complex line of theological argumentation. (Interestingly it is a line of argumentation that has been employed against premillennialism as a whole).[116] Since premillennialism takes the 1000 years of Revelation 20 literally, it must recognize the presence of unbelievers in the

---

[116] Floyd Hamilton, *The Basis of Millennial Faith* (Grand Rapids: Eerdmans, 1942), 137.

millennial earth as well as that of believers because there is a rebellion at the conclusion of the millennium. Obviously, glorified believers will not produce such a rebellion, and both resurrected and translated believers will be glorified. Where will these unconverted rebels come from? According to this argument, an interval of time must transpire in order for conversions to occur among those who are not taken and glorified in the Rapture and yet will, as believers, enter the millennium. In order to understand the pre-tribulationists' effort to find support here it will be helpful once again to state the argument syllogistically.

> ***Major Premise*:** There is a rebellion at the end of the millennium. Believers will not rebel.
>
> ***Minor Premise*:** Only believers enter the millennium — some of whom must remain in natural bodies in order to provide unconverted offspring who rebel.
>
> ***Conclusion*:** The Rapture must occur before the Advent in order to provide an interval of time for Tribulation saints to be converted subsequent to the Rapture and enter the millennium in natural bodies.

One should pause to observe that this argument, even if successful, would still not establish pre-tribulationism since each of the mid-tribulational positions and the partial Rapture theory would meet its demands. The success of this argument simply removes the viability of post-tribulationism, which seems to be the motivating factor in its presentation.

Feinberg states that some post-tribulationists have been unaware of this supposed problem for their viewpoint.[117] While he leaves this undocumented, it is plausible to suggest that such an omission in post-tribulational literature may occur due to the later appearance of this argument in the evolution of pre-tribulational polemics. However, post-tribulationists who have written in response to the argument point out numerous passages which appear to contradict the minor premise which requires that only believers enter the millennium.[118] Some of the passages that indicate that the unsaved will enter the millennium follow. In Zechariah 14:16-17 the prophet speaks of a remnant left of the nations that come against Jerusalem at the climax of the Tribulation:

> *And it shall come to pass that all they which are left of the nations which came against Jerusalem shall even go up from year to year to worship...whoso will not come up...upon them shall be no rain.*

In his description of events surrounding Christ's rescue of Israel at the close of the Tribulation, Ezekiel speaks of "the heathen that are left round about you" (36:36). Daniel speaks of some of the colleagues of the Beast remaining when he says: "As concerning the rest of the beasts, they had their dominion taken away; yet their lives were prolonged for a

---

[117] Feinberg, "Case," 73.

[118] Gundry, *Church,* 166-171. See also William E. Bell, *A Critical Evaluation of the Pretribulation Rapture Doctrine in Christian Eschatology* (Ph. D. dissertation, NYU, 1967), 247-248.

season" (7:12). Isaiah speaks of those remaining after Israel is exalted in the millennial earth when he says: "The sons also of them that afflicted thee shall come bending unto thee" (60:14). Each of these texts imply the presence of the unconverted in the millennial earth. The list could be expanded.

Feinberg, wrestling with Gundry and Bell on this point, admits but attempts to deflect the significance of their observations by distinguishing between the mere existence of the unconverted in the millennium and their *entrance* into the millennium.[119] That is, he admits the agreed prospect of the ungodly being present during the millennium, but he denies their presence at the beginning of the millennium. But this seems clearly incompatible with the statements about these ungodly being "left" or of their being comprised of a remnant remaining from the nations which came against Israel during the Tribulation. He rests his case upon the understanding that the judgment of the nations outlined in Matthew 25 occurs and is completed at the beginning of the millennium. This leaves only believers to *enter* at the beginning of the kingdom. Gundry observes that the judgment rendered in Matthew 25 indicates a post-millennial time frame, thus identifying it with the judgment of Revelation 20.[120] Feinberg rejects this and points to a temporal indicator referring to the beginning of the

[119] "Case," 75.

[120] *Church,* 166f.

millennium in Matthew 25:31 which reads: "when the Son of Man comes in his glory." This has weight, but the problem is that this sequence which sees the judgment of Matthew 25 occurring at the beginning of the millennium really presents more of a problem for the whole system of premillennialism than it does for post-tribulationism since the judgment rendered seems to point to the eternal state. This would bring the Second Advent and the eternal state together. Moo wrestles with this observation in his rebuttal to Feinberg and suggests that this is an instance of the common scriptural phenomenon of prophetic telescoping. "All premillennialists recognize that Scripture often blends together events that precede and follow the Millennium (cf. John 5:29; Jude 14-15)."[121] This seems to be a consistent answer to the common premillennial problem of Matthew 25, but it also removes the support sought by pre-tribulationists from the passage. If pre-tribulationists seek support from Matthew 25 then they must remove any post-millennial aspect to the *eternal* sentence pronounced. Insisting upon the pre-millennial time frame for this judgment leaves pre-tribulationism with the necessity of an *additional* judgment for the unbelievers that do *exist* in the millennium as referenced earlier. Again, pre-tribulationists usually argue that the Great White Throne only includes the unrighteous *dead*. This would not include the *living* ungodly from the Millennium. So yet another

[121] Moo, "Response," 162-163.

duplication/multiplication of an event becomes necessary for the pre-tribulationist.

Beyond his key resting point of the judgment of Matthew 25, Feinberg additionally argues that *righteousness* is a requirement for entering the kingdom and cites Matthew 5:20, Matthew 7:21, and John 3:3 as evidence.[122] In these passages one reads of the need for individual righteousness to exceed the righteousness of the Scribes and Pharisees to enter the kingdom (Matt. 5), of the fact that not everyone who calls Christ Lord will enter the Kingdom (Matt. 7), and of the necessity of being born again to enter the kingdom (John 3). But these passages seem clearly to speak of the common and more general reference to the Kingdom of God in its current individual, spiritual, and soteriological manifestations and not to speak of the eschatological earthly reign as Feinberg weakly suggests. Thus no support is found for the specific demands of the minor premise that only believers enter the millennium as demanded by the pre-tribulational argument. These texts speak of the "already" aspect of the spiritual Kingdom of God, not the "not yet" eschatological millennial kingdom.

One final thought deserves mention before drawing this section to a close. One could actually grant both the major and the minor premises of this theological syllogism and this would still not remove the viability of post-tribulationism.

[122] Feinberg, "Case," 76.

National Israel could still meet the requirement of a believing non-glorified people who are present and enter at the very beginning of the millennium if it were true that only believers enter at the commencement of the reign. If the mass conversion within National Israel at the Second Advent (that all premillennialists expect) occurs after the gathering of the resurrected righteous and the translation of living saints, they could enter the millennial earth without being glorified. Their looking in faith upon the one whom they pierced could happen while he visibly descends with his gathered people. This could be the culminating event of their being provoked to jealousy. Without endorsing this outline of events, this is simply offered to show that even when each premise of the necessary syllogism upon which this argument rests is granted, it *still* falls short of proving its intended conclusion of making a post-tribulation Rapture impossible.

Conclusion

Arguments based upon the supposed "necessity of an interval" between the Rapture and the Second Advent represent some of the most complex theological maneuvering in the whole Rapture debate and yet these maneuverings prove unsuccessful. The complexity was introduced by an evolving presentation of the pre-tribulational doctrine and is not present in the simple

Historic Premillennial perspective. One should again observe that the endeavors collected under this category seek merely to nullify post-tribulationism rather than supplying positive evidence for pre-tribulationism. Sifting through the layers of argumentation neither the Judgment Seat of Christ, nor the Marriage Supper of the Lamb, nor the Population of the Millennium can rise to the level of providing evidence for an additional coming of Christ. None of these meets the demands of "good and necessary consequence" for theological conclusions to be drawn. None of them reflects a natural or a plausible exposition of the passages involved. Each of them creates more problems than their proponents intend.

Chapter 7

IS THE CHURCH THE RESTRAINER?

The next major proof offered by pre-tribulationists lies in the belief that the NT church must be removed from the earth before the Antichrist can be revealed. This focuses thought on the "restrainer" of 2 Thessalonians 2:6-7. While based upon an offered exegesis, the uncertainty of the passage will also leave this argument resting upon theological inference rather than clear exposition. The usual pre-tribulational construction of the passage follows this outline: Paul writes to assure some questioning Thessalonians that the Day of the Lord had not yet arrived. Certain things must happen first. There will be a "falling away," and the Man of Sin will be revealed, and the Man of Sin cannot be revealed until the NT church is "taken out of the way."

The pre-tribulationist E. Schuyler English suggested that the "falling away" (*apostasia*) of vs. 3 is the "departure" of the NT church in the Rapture. [123] A small minority has followed English and suggested that this is the scripture's only direct statement of pre-tribulationism. The fact that a majority even within pre-tribulationism refuses to accept this interpretation of the "falling away" indicates the strain and bias it reflects, [124] though Walvoord still includes it conditionally among his "Fifty Reasons."[125] Parallel passages and normal usage of the language lead heavily to the conclusion that ecclesiastical apostasy is in view and not the church's departure from the earth. Also this interpretation seems to be impossible considering that vs. 1 already references "our gathering together unto Him." This gathering at His "coming" surely refers to the Rapture and supplies one of the three key references to the event described earlier. Given English's innovative exposition Paul would be left saying: "The Rapture cannot happen until after the Rapture happens."

Far more widely accepted is the suggestion that the removal of the "restrainer" of vs. 6-7 somehow indicates the Rapture. Few would present the straightforward claim that the NT church is the restrainer. The more common pre-tribulational assertion identifies the restraint as a peculiar presence of the Holy Spirit during the NT church age. Given

---

[123] E. Schuyler English, "Rethinking the Rapture," *Our Hope* 56 (May 1950): 650-666.

[124] D. Edmond Hiebert, *The Thessalonian Epistles* (Chicago: Moody Press, 1971), 306. See Reiter, "Development," 32.

[125] Walvoord, *Question*, 196.

the impossibility of the removal of an omnipresent being, the usual presentation of the argument involves suggesting a reversion to an Old Testament economy where, upon a Dispensational understanding, believers were not indwelt by the Spirit. Thus post-Rapture Tribulation saints, also not indwelt, pose no such restraint and Antichrist can be revealed once the Spiritually indwelt body has been taken out of the way. This has become normative within pre-tribulationism. Walvoord is representative:

> The most natural explanation...is to identify this particular action with the time when Christ will come to take out His church. If the Spirit of God indwells the church and the church is taken out of the world, then the Spirit of God will also be taken out of the world. This does not mean that the Spirit will not continue working in the world in some way; but it will mean a reversal of Pentecost.[126]

Ryrie agrees and answers objections by parsing between the Spirit's *residence* and his *presence.*[127] Stanton reaches beyond Walvoord's suggestion that this is the "most natural explanation" and claims that the restrainer is "undoubtedly the Holy Spirit."[128]

The reader should pause before proceeding and consider some of the ramifications of this suggestion. This most popular pre-tribulational argument from this passage

---

[126] Walvoord, *Thessalonians*, 125-126.

[127] Ryrie, *First and Second Thessalonians* (Chicago: Moody Press, 1959), 113. Also see Stanton, *Kept*, 105.

[128] Stanton, *Kept*, 106.

views the removal of the NT church and the beginning of the Tribulation as a reversion back to an OT economy. If one were to grant the Dispensational suggestion that OT believers were not indwelt by the Spirit (which is not being granted),[129] proponents usually seek to support this assertion with the claim that the full indwelling of the Spirit was not possible until Christ had been raised from the dead and had sent forth this fullness of the Spirit upon the NT church following his ascension. But no such limitation will exist for Tribulation saints. Christ's resurrection and ascension will not be rescinded prior to the beginning of the Tribulation. If this necessity and the lack of the historical completion of Christ's work supplies the reason why OT saints were not indwelt by the Spirit (according to the Dispensational teaching), what reality or what motivation can be supplied for withholding the fullness of the Spirit from any category of NT believers when the necessity and lack of the historical completion of Christ's redemptive work no longer applies? Dispensationalists have a hard case to prove in this aspect of their suggested reversion back to an OT state of affairs, but, as with many of the difficulties their argumentation introduces, they fail to address this ramification of their teaching. Once again, the reader should notice the

[129] One can understand the fact of a greater fullness of the Spirit being granted in the outpouring for the new age that began at Pentecost without suggesting that OT believers were not indwelt by the Spirit. Greater light, greater fullness, and greater spiritual power do not imply of necessity no light, no indwelling and no spiritual power for the OT people.

inevitability of soteriological problems arising once the presuppositions of Dispensationalism are granted. But returning to the issue at hand, one must ask, are these inferences from the text valid? A brief examination of this admittedly difficult passage is in order.

Non-Dispensational writers have lacked such confidence in identifying the restrainer. The passage has puzzled commentators from the earliest times. Augustine confessed that after great pains he was unable to make the identification.[130] In his commentary Richard Wolff offers a good historical summary of the various interpretations of the passage and highlights seven suggestions that have emerged.[131] A list of these seven interpretations with some comments interspersed follows. (1) Some have suggested that the existence of the Jewish state served to offer protection to the church thus it should be seen as the restrainer. But Wolff concludes that "this view of Benjamin B. Warfield can hardly be justified in the light of 1 Thess. 2:14-16 or the events of history." This preterist view also places the events in the past. This is hardly acceptable to premillennialists. (2) Wolff calls the view that Nero was the Antichrist and that the restraining power was Vespasian and Titus a "historical curiosity." This preterist interpretation should perhaps be quickly dismissed as well. (3) Strangely

---

[130] *City of God*, XX, xix.

[131] Richard Wolff, *Thessalonians* (Wheaton, Illinois: Tyndale House, 1970), 84-87.

enough some have suggested that Satan is the Restrainer. But this necessitates translating "restrain" as "holding sway" which is highly unlikely given that the appearance of Antichrist is delayed until the activity in question ends. It also involves making a difficult link between the phrase "taken out of the way" and Satan's being cast out of heaven (Rev. 12:7). (4) Some have envisioned an unnamed angelic power similar to that described in Daniel 10 which restrained the prince of Persia. (5) Some have offered a more general opinion that the Divine decree is that which restrains, but this labors under the difficulty of explaining how the eternal decree can be "taken out of the way." It also seems unnatural to refer to such an obvious but general truth under such specific language. The decree obviously lies underneath whatever the specific reference intends to identify, but something more specific certainly lies behind the reference. (6) Chrysostom referenced some in his day who suggested that the "grace of the Spirit" was the restrainer. This he argued was impossible due to the cessation of the Charismatic gifts. Interestingly Wolff sees similarity in this very old suggestion to the Dispensational assertion of the uniqueness of the Spirit's presence within church saints, but he offers his this critique:

> To assume that after the rapture of the church the activity of the Holy Spirit will be similar to his ministry before the day of Pentecost hardly does

> justice to the words "out of the way" indicating removal and not a mere change in operation.[132]

(7) Historically the most prevalent view has identified the restrainer as the Roman Empire. After his aforementioned confession of uncertainty, Augustine commended this interpretation. In the passage Paul refers to previous oral instruction that had identified the restrainer when he clearly remarked that the Thessalonians already knew what restrained (vs. 6). The fact that Paul declined to identify the restrainer in the *written* epistle actually becomes part of the argument for this popular historic interpretation. Making a written comment about the political power of the day might at some point prove dangerous for those who possessed a copy of the letter. After completing his survey, Wolff cautiously endorses this view:

> This seems to be the most satisfactory view because it explains (1) Paul's reticence to name the power, (2) the quasi-unanimous tradition of the early church and (3) fits into the context which speaks of...lawlessness as the basic principle of the antichrist.[133]

To Wolff's list of seven interpretations the inquirer should also add (8) Calvin's view of the "career of the gospel." Light was to "be diffused through all parts of the earth before God

---

[132] Wolff, *Thessalonians,* 85.

[133] Wolff, *Thessalonians,* 86.

would give loose reins to Satan."[134] And finally, Hendriksen endorses the view of Ellicott (9) that "well ordered human rule" supplies the restraint.[135]

It is possible to take this last interpretation as an extension or a variation of the widespread interpretation that the restrainer was the Roman Empire. Rome was but the contemporary expression of civil authority when Paul wrote to the Thessalonians. Most premillennialists view Rome, or a "revived Roman empire" as the last stage of Gentile power in the important prophetic image of Daniel chapter 2. It could be that the failure or declension of this final stage of the "times of the Gentiles" paves the way for the reign of Antichrist. One of the benefits of well ordered human rule, and a reason for believers to pray for those who hold civil authority is that "we might lead a quiet and peaceable life" (1 Tim. 2:2). In the absence of such an ordered civil authority, history has shown the possibility of one man usurping unprecedented powers and the possible use of lawlessness (due to the absence or weakness of current civil powers) to gain such power or to advance a radical agenda.

There is an additional reason to weigh this variation of the ancient interpretation heavily. The phrase translated

---

[134] John Calvin *Calvin's Commentaries* Vol. XXI (Grand Rapids: Baker, 1979 reprint), 333. For a contemporary defense of this view (linked with #4) see Kim Riddlebarger, *The Man of Sin* (Grand Rapids: Baker Books, 2006), 130-134.

[135] William Hendriksen, *New Testament Commentary: Thessalonians, Timothy and Titus* (Grand Rapids: Baker, 1979), 181.

"taken out of the way" in the Authorized Version has been challenged by exegetes. William Hendriksen—no friend to Dispensationalism—defends the translation "taken out of the way" in the face of challenges,[136] but some have suggested that *ek mesou ginetai* should more literally read "becomes [arises] out of the midst." The phrase concerning the restrainer could thus become parenthetical and the verse read as B. W. Newton translates:

> *For the mystery of lawlessness doth already work (only there is one at present that restraineth) until it becomes developed out of the midst, and then shall the Lawless one be revealed.*[137]

The focus of the passage then becomes Paul's assurance that the mystery which is now working in the background in its opposition to Christ, will, in the final form of the mystery, *rising out of the midst* of its developing predecessors, culminate in the appearance of the Man of Lawlessness in the last days.

An attractive parallel occurs when one weds the interpretation of civil authority as the restrainer to this translation which finds Antichrist "arising out of the midst." One of Daniel's descriptions of the Antichrist is the "little horn" (7:8) that *arises from among* the ten horns of the fourth beast, which according to premillennial interpretation is the last phase of Gentile power. If indeed restraint occurs

[136] Hendriksen, *Thessalonians,* 181.

[137] Newton, *Prospects,* 212.

through civil governments until God allows Antichrist to arise out of the midst of these corrupting rulers, then the sequence in 2 Thessalonians 2:6-7 would not be *restraint* until the *removal* (of the restrainer) as is commonly held, but *restraint* until the *revelation* (of the Antichrist).[138] This also fits well with the context which in vs. 3-5 and vs. 8-10 speaks specifically and descriptively of the manner in which the Man of Sin, "that Wicked," shall be *revealed*.

Leaving these competing perspectives on the identity of the restrainer aside, as well as leaving aside this suggestion that phrase thought to indicate the removal of the restrainer could actually refer to the revelation of Antichrist (thus the passage actually *omits* any specific reference to the restraint being removed), the question remains, what of the viability of the pre-tribulational argument? This becomes a *tenth*, and a *minority* interpretation. (Given its recent introduction, this interpretation arguably arises from a preexisting pre-tribulationism rather than pre-tribulationism arising from this preexisting interpretation). Seeking support for a doctrine on a difficult and unspecified reference, especially one that is so variously interpreted, and perhaps intentionally vague, proves the height of folly, especially considering the leaps that are necessary to achieve the desired end. The first leap is the debated interpretation that

---

[138] While Newton does not suggest the link with the "Little Horn," my thoughts leading to this analysis are developed from his *Prospects*, 100-101 and 212-215.

the Spirit is the restrainer. Some think with Hendriksen that this is impossible "even on the surface."[139] The second, and huge, leap occurs when the suggestion demands that the means whereby the Spirit ends the restraint is the physical removal of believers from the earth. A third, and troubling, leap occurs when this interpretation limits this restraining influence to the saints of the current dispensation while demanding that the saints of the days immediately following cannot possess the same spiritual position. Upon this inference, without regard to the formidable questions involved, Pentecost almost casually remarks:

> Since all of the Spirit's ministries to the believer today depend upon His indwelling presence, the absence of this prevents all the dependent ministries to the tribulation saints.[140]

Even assuming the viability of the second leap and the inability of Tribulational Israel (while in unbelief) to provide this restraint, there is no justification for the Dispensationalists' demand of such spiritual difference between NT church saints and Tribulation saints. A further inconsistency appears when pre-tribulationists suggest that it is the spiritually weak church of the last days (with or without the 'Laodicean Age' interpretation from the letters to the churches in Revelation 2-3) which provides the restraining influence that holds back the strongest

---

[139] Hendriksen, *Thessalonians,* 181.

[140] Pentecost, *Things,* 263.

manifestation of evil the world will ever witness. Even on pre-tribulational terms, Tribulation saints will arguably exhibit greater spiritual power than the pre-tribulational church which this interpretation credits for the restraint.

The demands placed upon this difficult and intentionally cryptic passage by pre-tribulationism are too great. This is amplified by the additional realities that no other passage suggests or supports the interpretation; that the interpretation represents a minority viewpoint on a passage with numerous possible interpretations; that the interpretation itself rests upon theological inferences that are highly questionable; and that once embraced these inferences introduce yet more soteriological problems. This passage falls far short of providing credible evidence for an additional coming of Christ. In fact, the context, as a later chapter will show, militates strongly against the pre-tribulational viewpoint.

Chapter 8

IS THERE A DISTINCTION BETWEEN TWO DIFFERENT FUTURE COMINGS?

Earlier it was suggested that although published arguments for pre-tribulationism extended to lists of great length, serious arguments should be limited to five. Having devoted four chapters to those appearing to carry the most weight, this chapter seeks briefly to sum up the remaining evidence. A common denominator of this additional evidence lies in the propensity for pre-tribulationists to distinguish scriptures that others view together. If the distinctions prove unwarranted, then evidence for pre-tribulationism once again fails. If scripture links the events then evidence for post-tribulationism, which already labors under no burden of proof, seems all the more convincing.

Pre-tribulationists have drawn much attention to some supposed contrasts between the Rapture and the Second

Advent. Twelve of Walvoord's "Fifty Reasons" appear in a section devoted to this. Just one example from these twelve, however, illustrates the *non sequitur* reasoning profoundly displayed throughout the rest. For one of these "reasons" Walvoord asserts: "The rapture concerns only the saved, while the second coming deals with both saved and unsaved."[141] The fact that only believers participate in the Rapture cannot substantiate the claim that this event occurs at a different time than other events. There is simply no scriptural or logical warrant for the suggestion. Further, as discussed below, clear scriptural evidence exists to the contrary. Pentecost's enumeration of these supposed distinctions between the Rapture and the Second Advent extends to seventeen. The first of his list reads: "The translation entails the removal of all believers, while the second advent entails the appearing or manifestation of the Son."[142] The fact that believers are gathered to meet Christ in the air at his coming does not preclude Christ from being publically revealed during the event. This is an incredible deduction. It is frankly hard to believe that such reasoning survived the editing, supervision, and examining process of a doctoral dissertation and the revision involved in its subsequent publication. No improvement appears in the remainder of Pentecost's list, which he actually states could be extended! Adding to these weak suggestions by his

---

[141] Walvoord, *Question,*199.

[142] Pentecost, *Things,* 206.

colleagues, Stanton argues that one should understand distinct locations for the Rapture and the Advent, one in the air and one on the earth, as evidence of two separate events.[143] But if there is a gathering of the church in the air to meet Christ as he returns through the air to the earth, then this insistence of two distinct events based upon two distinct locations becomes the height of folly. It is simply biased, gratuitous, and illogical.

These are not isolated missteps by obscure pre-tribulationists. These were the spokesmen for the system during days of its fiercest and most celebrated defense. Illustrations of such argumentation could be multiplied from numerous authors. It is almost embarrassing to highlight such reasoning by recognized authorities. None of the multiplied distinctions which these writers suggest demands or even implies the separation of the Rapture and the Advent.

This leaves one remaining thought to bring the survey of the evidence for an additional coming of Christ to a close. Perhaps the most foundational issue lies not in seeking to prove there is a distinction between the Rapture and the Second Advent, but in assuming the distinction between Israel and the NT church as taught by classical Dispensationalism. The debate between Covenant Theology and Dispensational Theology has already been referenced as

---

[143] Stanton, *Kept*, 265.

a necessary companion study in understanding the Rapture debate within premillennialism. The previous survey illustrates that the attempt to supply evidence for an additional coming of Christ fails on its own merit. If the nature of the distinction between Israel and the NT church as demanded by Dispensationalism fails, then not only does most of the argumentation for pre-tribulationism fail under scrutiny, as illustrated in the preceding chapters, it disappears altogether. It was only in bringing this presupposition alongside the scriptural passages in question that made the pre-tribulational offerings of exposition possible.

It is true that all premillennialists must see some measure of distinction for National Israel if there is to be a future for the nation in the millennial kingdom. How Gentile believers relate to that kingdom can be discussed among premillennialists without doing damage to the overall premillennial system. But the distinctions between Israel and the NT church that Darby introduced reach beyond the temporal and administrative distinctions recognized by Historic Premillennialism. They reach into the spiritual and organic realms. As a result, Dispensationalism has constantly been on the defensive from serious critics because of the soteriological problems it introduces. As already noted, this larger debate reaches beyond the limited scope of this book. Inquirers should refer to the works mentioned throughout the footnotes to pursue these larger questions. A few comments on the topic, however, may be helpful to spur interest in that direction.

It was reading of the glories and heavenly position of the church, particularly as described in the epistle to the Ephesians, that gave rise to Darby's novel interpretations regarding the distinction between Israel and the NT church, which in turn provided the foundation for Dispensational theology. During a period of convalescence from an injury, Darby reflected upon the lofty standing of the church as being joined to Christ and seated in the heavenlies. He saw this position as distinct from believers in the OT dispensation. He further came to see the necessity of abandoning all confidence in his own works. He again saw this to be in *contrast* to the requirements of those in the OT dispensation.[144] The outworkings of this fundamental premise are displayed in the writings of L. S. Chafer and C. I. Scofield which have come under such serious challenge for their implications (and some would argue direct statements) regarding salvation by works in the OT and salvation by grace in the NT.[145]

In the following generation Charles Ryrie was charged with providing a defense of his predecessors, but his revision of the system failed. Evidence for the failure of the system

---

[144] For a survey of the history of Darby's thinking see Fuller, *Hermeneutics*, 38f.

[145] See the works cited in footnote 2 and especially Kimbro, *Dispensationalism*, 93-130.

seems to be clearly displayed in the fact that the next generation of scholars (within the very institutions founded by Dispensationalism) found it necessary to revise the system yet again and put forward "Progressive Dispensationalism" in direct contradiction to the key demands of both generations of their predecessors. The foundational tenet of the newer revision was their admission that rather than the sharp distinction between Israel and the NT church that the previous Dispensationalists had claimed, the scriptures instead describe a continuity between Israel and the NT church. As these men became committed to more careful exegesis, the theological conclusions of the previous generations were abandoned, yet adding to the confusion of the contemporary church (as discussed in the opening chapter of this book) these men still want to keep the title "Dispensationalism" for their viewpoint, when all they really continue to defend is premillennialism.

But if the sharp, and soteriological, distinctions between Israel and the NT church that were introduced by the framers and defenders of Dispensational theology fail under scrutiny (as friend and foe alike now seem to be recognizing), then the key foundation for pre-tribulationism is taken away. It has been evident in examining every proof that is offered for the pre-tribulational Rapture that this single theological presupposition has provided the motivation and the underpinning. It has also provided every *difficulty* that has been exposed in the previous scrutiny of their suggested evidence.

Before closing this chapter, I would like to include a brief portion of an argument from my earlier book which has been cited, and that from a section dealing with the scriptural evidence for the unity of the people of God.[146]

Perhaps the most explicit scriptures touching upon this issue occur in the book of Ephesians.

> *Wherefore remember, that ye being in time past Gentiles in the flesh, who are called Uncircumcision by that which is called the Circumcision in the flesh made by hands; That at that time ye were without Christ, being aliens from the commonwealth of Israel, and strangers from the covenants of promise, having no hope, and without God in the world: But now in Christ Jesus ye who sometimes were far off are made nigh by the blood of Christ. For he is our peace, who hath made both one, and hath broken down the middle wall of partition between us (2:11-14).*

The Dispensationalists utilize this passage in their attempts to define the church as a new phenomenon, yet it specifically contradicts their claims. The above scripture reminds Gentile converts that they were brought from a lost and helpless condition to their glorious position in Christ. Paul's wording is specific. These Gentiles had been a*t one time* "aliens" and "strangers," but now in Christ they are no longer aliens and

[146] Kimbro, *Dispensationalism*, 75-77.

strangers. They have been brought near. What have they been brought near to? What were they formerly aliens to that now they are joined with? Clearly the answer is that they are now part of *the commonwealth of Israel, the covenants of promise.* God in his sovereign plan has sent the gospel unto them that they might partake of the blessings which heretofore only Israel had possessed. (Paul also stated this early privilege of the Jews in Romans 3:1-2, where, after showing the equal footing of the Jews and Gentiles morally before God, he says, "What advantage then hath the Jew? Or what profit is there of circumcision? Much every way chiefly, because that unto them were committed the oracles of God.") Now, the good news of Christ—one and the same with the message of the Old Testament—is being sent to the Gentiles as well.

Ephesians 2:11 makes a remarkable statement in reference to the Ephesians. They had been "in time past Gentiles." The obvious inference is that there is a sense in which they are not Gentiles anymore. They are now, spiritually speaking, part of the "commonwealth of Israel." "Now therefore ye are no more strangers and foreigners, but fellowcitizens with the saints, and of the household of God" (vs. 19).

How then do the Dispensationalists interpret this passage? In his book on premillennialism, Ryrie gives this explanation of the same verses:

> In this passage Gentiles are expressly said to be excluded from the blessings peculiar to Israel. In going on to state their blessings in the church, Paul does not say that once having believed, these Gentiles now come into the Israelite blessings, but rather that God has brought about a new thing, the new man in Christ Jesus.[147]

This is indeed strained exegesis to prove a preconceived idea. How is it possible to conclude that Paul's language communicates something from which the Ephesians were "excluded." The whole passage proclaims the good news that they were "brought near." Though clumsy grammatically, the following accurately paraphrases Ryrie's treatment of the passage:

> "You were once far away, but are now brought near—to something new and totally distinct from that from which you are still far away."

This is obviously not what Paul is saying. Presumably, according to Ryrie's reading of his system into the passage, the comfort for the Ephesians lies in the superior and disconnected nature of the new economy to which they belong. But this exposes the thorny question of Dispensationalism's doctrine of salvation again.

These Dispensational conclusions also draw upon their unique understanding of the way in which the NT church was a mystery hidden from past ages. But the mystery Paul references in Ephesians is not the introduction of a new and

[147] Ryrie, *Basis, 64.*

unconnected body of people, as Dispensationalism claims, but rather the revelation that Gentiles would be "fellow heirs and of the same body" (3:6). Their "engrafting" into the *one* olive tree (Romans 11), only slightly foreshadowed in the OT, has come into full and vibrant experience.

These passages are but a sampling. The abundant scriptural evidence for the essential unity of the saints of all ages argues against Darby's defining distinction between Israel and the NT church. This newly introduced *spiritual* level of Dispensational distinction moves far beyond the previous level of *administrative* and *ceremonial* distinctions recognized by Historic Premillennialists. Remove the theological presupposition of Darby's definition of the NT church and the argument for a pre-tribulation Rapture disappears.

Chapter 9

ADDITIONAL POSITIVE EVIDENCE FOR HISTORIC PREMILLENNIALISM

It follows now to conclude with a brief survey of some of the positive scriptural evidence for viewing the Rapture and the Second Advent as occurring at the same time. The previous chapter addressed the pre-tribulational claims of the distinctions between the Rapture and the Advent. This chapter will address the scriptural evidence for bringing the two together. One should remember that no burden of proof rests upon the Historic Premillennial position. If evidence for teaching an additional coming of Christ is lacking, then of necessity all of the events surrounding the second coming of Christ occur at the *one* second coming. But positive evidence for the post-tribulation Rapture is not lacking.

Decisive evidence for the coincidence of the Rapture and the Second Advent has already been offered in the survey of the resurrection in chapter 3 of this book. One also finds that Paul's teaching in 2 Thessalonians 1 enhances the same understanding of the time sequence discovered there. In comforting the suffering Thessalonians, Paul instructs them that when the "Lord Jesus shall be revealed from heaven with his mighty angels" their persecutors will be recompensed with tribulation and fiery judgment while they will be recompensed with rest and glory (vs. 6-7). These occur at the same time, when Christ is *revealed* from heaven. When Dispensationalists admit that this must refer to the Second Advent but add (without any contextual evidence) that the Rapture must have occurred previously[148] they fail to answer the difficulty incumbent within their strained exegesis, that the promised rest and glory of the believers would then be recompensed seven years *after* their supposed rapture to heaven. Nor do they answer the seemingly insurmountable difficulty that the Thessalonian, NT, Gentile believers are left *watching* for the clearly post-tribulational event of the Lord's Second Advent in which this fiery judgment of the ungodly occurs. It is also at this same coming that the Lord is "glorified in his saints and admired among all them that believe" (vs. 10). All of this indicates a post-tribulational expectation for the Thessalonians.

Reading further into 2 Thessalonians, as noted already, 2 Thessalonians 2:1 states that the "gathering together" of

---

[148] Walvoord, *Thessalonians*, 108-110.

believers unto Christ occurs at his coming. This must refer to the Rapture. That this event is referenced again in the following verse as the "day of Christ" seems evident. And if this is the case, as appears obvious, it is clear that the thrust of the following verses intends to educate the Thessalonians that "that day" cannot come until after the intervening events of the great apostasy and the career of Antichrist. This seems clearly to place the Rapture after the Tribulation. Further, Christ's "coming" is mentioned twice in the passage. In vs. 1 it is linked with "our gathering together unto him." In vs. 8 it is linked with the destruction of the Antichrist. No distinction or intention to indicate two separate comings appears in the passage at all. Much to the contrary, finding two different comings separated by the seven year Tribulation does violence to the context.

Next, one finds that a comparison between an event described in a portion of the Olivet Discourse (Matthew 24: 29-31) and the key Rapture passage (1 Thessalonians 4: 16-17) reveals an impressive list of parallels:

Matthew 24	**I Thessalonians 4**
Son of Man	*The Lord Himself*
Clouds	*Clouds*
His angels	*Voice of the Archangel*
Sound of a Trumpet	*The Trump of God*
Gather together His Elect	*Caught up together*

Matthew explicitly references a post-tribulational gathering of the elect at the coming of the Son of Man. Thessalonians clearly describes the Rapture at the coming of the Lord himself. It would seem that a definitive scriptural reason would be necessary to conclude that these passages refer to two different events. The usual pre-tribulational answer unfolds in the demand that one be viewed as Jewish and the other Christian.[149] But this theological maneuver is fraught with difficulties and strained explanations such as limiting "the elect" to Israel and causing a virtual schizophrenia to descend upon the listening disciples in determining which discourses—or portions of the same discourse!—view them as representing Israel and which view them as representing the NT church. (This is the same introduction of a presupposition into the passage without warrant that has prevailed throughout the discussion). Also, these parallels between Matthew and Thessalonians become more impressive when comparing them with the unfolding of the seventh trumpet in Revelation 11. The details surrounding the sounding of the seventh trumpet (if the following chapters are parenthetical) actually include the entire list from the parallels between Matthew and Thessalonians. There the reader finds in addition to the sounding of the "trumpet:" "One like unto the Son of Man," sitting upon a "white cloud," an "angel crying with a loud voice," and the

---

[149] A. C. Gaebelein, *The Olivet Discourse* (Grand Rapids: Baker, 1969 reprint), 8-9.

earth being "reaped" (14: 14-16). It is also impressive to add to these observations the "great trumpet" appearing in Isaiah's "mini-apocalypse" (27:13) where the resurrection figured so prominently as previously discussed, and the "last trump" of 1 Corinthians 15:52 which of course fulfills the prophecy of Isaiah as Paul explicitly teaches. 1 Corinthians 15 also clearly describes the same events as 1 Thessalonians 4 where the resurrection and translation of believers are brought together. Also the added description of the trumpet in 1 Corinthians as the "last" trump leads to the question of what sequence of trumpets this trumpet of the resurrection is the "last" of? The series of seven trumpets in Revelation seems to provide an unrivaled answer for this question.

Understanding that the seventh trumpet occurs at the close of the Tribulation presents an obvious difficulty for pre-tribulationism, so most pre-tribulationists refuse to place the trumpet at that time and argue against a cyclical view of the Seals, Trumpets, and Bowls in the book. But it seems obvious that the seventh trumpet occurs at the close of the Tribulation because when it sounds the proclamation is made, "the kingdoms of this world are become the kingdoms of our Lord and of his Christ; and he shall reign for ever and ever" (11:15). Ryrie weakly by-passes this difficulty in his commentary by saying:

> ...the meaning is that the dominion of the world is taken over by Christ. Some additional events have to

transpire before all is realized, but the end is near and now the announcement can be made.[150]

Next, an important word study in the classic Rapture passage (1 Thessalonians 4:17) reinforces the post-tribulational distinctive concerning the destination of believers following the Rapture and gives much help in determining the time of the event. It will perhaps be useful at this point to reintroduce a chart supplied earlier:

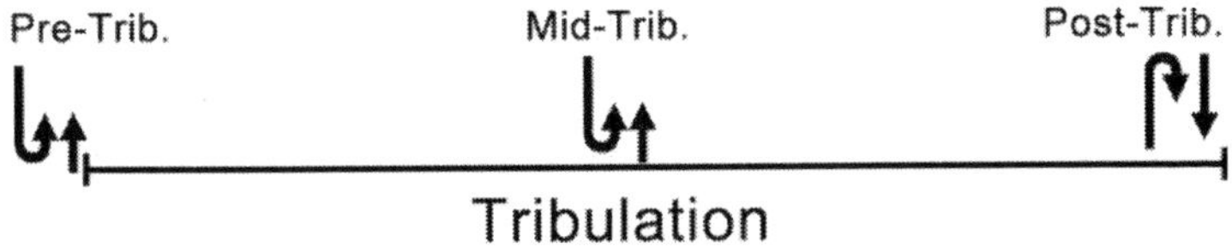

Remember, in all the other viewpoints Christ removes from heaven to the skies, gathers the church in the Rapture and then returns with the church to heaven for all or part of the Tribulation period. In the post-tribulational viewpoint, however, Christ returns from heaven to the earth and gathers the full church (both resurrected and translated) unto himself in the air *as he descends to the earth in glory* to gain the victory over the Man of Sin and set up his millennial reign. It is the church that returns to the place of origin in the event, not Christ.

One finds that the wording translated "*to meet* the Lord in the air" contains a vividly descriptive element that sheds light on this event. The Greek phrase (*eis apantesin*) often

---

150 *Revelation,* 75.

occurs as a technical expression for one going out to meet an approaching dignitary for the purpose of escorting that arriving dignitary back to his own place of origin. This would be similar to the mayor of a city going to the airport to welcome the President of the United States when he landed before travelling back with the President to the city for the scheduled event the President had arrived to attend. Secular Greek sources confirm this specialized use of the term. The other places in the New Testament where this term occurs also fit this specialized usage. In Matthew 25:1&6 the watching virgins go forth "to meet" the approaching bridegroom, with whom they will return to the wedding. Not only is this passage linguistically connected to 1 Thessalonians 4:17, it is paralleled in its eschatological context. In the other place where the wording occurs in the New Testament, Acts 28:15, the reader finds that some of the local believers went out to meet the Apostle Paul as he approached the city of Rome, for the purpose of escorting him back to the city he had so long waited to visit. Conforming to this uniform and specialized usage, 1 Thessalonians 4:17 then describes the Rapture as those saints who are alive at the Second Advent going forth at the shout of the angel and the sound of the trumpet "to meet" the approaching Christ and returning with him to the earth in his glorious appearing. This not only fits the post-tribulational outline of events, it seems a very natural interpretation of the passage—indeed more than natural and rather demanded if the specific meaning of this specialized wording is recognized. (And if not, this would be the only case in the NT where it did not apply). If the sole purpose of the Rapture is the removal of the church from the earth, again one might ask why Christ comes to the skies in order to accomplish this. He can easily bring the church to heaven without leaving heaven. But if the purpose of the meeting in the air is to welcome the Savior upon his return and to be publically identified with him in his glorious appearing this specialized term has great significance and fits seamlessly with all the other descriptions of the Advent and the public revelation of Christ in glory.

Another important observation occurs in 1 Thessalonians 5 and brings this brief final chapter to a close. This has been hinted at already on the title page of this book, but in this part of Paul's eschatological instruction to the Thessalonians he reminds them of truths that he was confident they already "knew perfectly" (vs. 2). Among these was the fact that the coming of Christ in the "Day of the Lord" will overtake the ungodly suddenly. This is because in their unbelief, and even the judicial blindness that God will have sent upon them as discussed earlier, they will be saying "peace and safety" during the reign of Antichrist, but in reality the troubles of those last days will come upon them in a fiery judgment when the Lord unexpectedly returns and that day overtakes them as a "thief in the night." But Paul speaks to the Thessalonian believers and says, "But ye, brethren, are not in darkness, that that day should overtake you as a thief" (vs. 4). He continues to affirm that the ungodly will be like the drunkard and not watchful, but rather in darkness, so the coming of Christ will be to them unexpected, but that the Thessalonian believers will be sober, watchful, and dwelling in the light, waiting for the *expected* appearance of Christ. The inescapable implication, indeed one should say the explicit reference in this passage is to the mutual presence of the godly Thessalonian Gentile NT church believers and the ungodly followers of Antichrist during the same days of Tribulation that will come upon the earth. The NT church believers will be present on earth for the arrival of that Day, it just won't overtake them as a thief like it will everybody else.

Conclusion

If popularity or best-sellers were the final court of appeals the pre-tribulational version of prophecy would doubtless win the day. If however the statements of scripture must settle the case, that majority of Evangelicals who hold and promote this viewpoint must become aware that foundation for this doctrine is entirely lacking. The key focus of this study has been to establish that the burden of proof within premillennialism rests upon all viewpoints except post-tribulationism to establish an additional coming of Christ, because it, contrary to the rest, holds to only one second coming. An analysis of the suggested evidence for the additional coming finds it to be insufficient in the highest degree. In fact the attempts to supply evidence for the additional coming introduce a host of exegetical and theological problems. With warrant for the additional coming lacking, one finds that the Historic Premillennial, post-tribulational, viewpoint accords best with scripture and also represents the simplest form of premillennialism.

Additional positive evidence for the Historic Premillennial view exists that is not presented in this book.

The leading post-tribulational writers make solid cases in exposition of their position. Readers are encouraged to take up these larger works and consider this topic further. This survey has primarily challenged the pre-tribulational accounting for its position and simply introduced the study of Historic Premillenialism. It is hoped that some will find food for thought concerning the Rapture, and perhaps even concerning some topics of much greater importance.

The nineteenth century saw the birth of Dispensational theology in the Brethren movement. The twentieth century saw the North American Evangelical and Fundamentalist movements permeated with its influence. In these circles pre-tribulationism became a *shibboleth* and the emotions surrounding debate on the topic ran high. In recent decades the rediscovery of Reformed Theology within broader Evangelical circles (and even more slowly in some Fundamentalist circles) together with the emergence of Progressive Dispensationalism within the most hallowed halls of Dispensationalism show evidence of a shift. Many within Dispensational circles are being attracted to historic Reformed theology but still draw a distinction between what they see as an erroneous Reformed eschatology and the premillennialism they wish to retain. In doing this they falsely limit a Reformed perspective to the opposing millennial viewpoints. Historic Premillennialism suffers from the paucity of current advocates and the prevalence of misinformation due to the widespread confusion of

Dispensationalism with premillennialism by nearly all parties following the evolution of Dispensational polemics in their desperate attempts at self-defense in the mid-twentieth century. It will be interesting to observe what effect this ongoing shift away from Dispensationalism has upon the ecclesiastical and eschatological landscape in the days ahead. It is hoped that Historic Premillennialism will gain a renewed hearing as the church moves forward.

The Apostle Peter spoke of scoffers arising in the last days and saying, "where is the promise of his coming?" (2 Peter 3:4). Could it be that at least some of these future scoffers will be, as so many of the unsaved have already become, aware of the widespread claims of the pre-tribulation Rapture and find additional occasion to mock when the trials of the Tribulation come upon the deceived world as well as upon the remaining church?

What also will become of both believers and professing believers who have been so exclusively taught that they will be taken out of the world before the Man of Sin appears on the scene or that great final persecution of God's people begins? What realities will emerge as many even in the professing church, so weak in their understanding of the Gospel, face the crafty and seemingly credible lies of the Antichrist? Confusion, disillusionment, and even apostasy (for the merely nominal Christian) could overtake many if the events of the 70th week begin to unfold while the church is still present to face the Beast as the early churchmen believed.

But doubtless, if the Historic Premillennial understanding is correct, the Lord will grant grace and spiritual help to believers while he dispenses "strong delusion" to the ungodly during that hour. In a text that is as sobering as it is comforting, our Lord said, "For there shall arise false Christs, and false prophets, and shall shew great signs and wonders; insomuch that, if it were possible, they shall deceive the very elect. Behold I have told you before." (Matt. 24:24-25). Surely that last generation of Christians will know by experience the *comfort* of which the Apostle wrote (1 Thess. 4:18 and 5:11) that that Day will not overtake them as a thief, like it will the ungodly.

It is hoped that this small volume will be of help to some who are willing to objectively examine the scriptures on this important subject and consider the possibility that we may all be "left behind."

BIBLIOGRAPHY

Augustine. City of God.

Barnhouse, Donald Gray. *Revelation.* Grand Rapids: Zondervan, 1971.

Beechick, Allen. *The Pre-Tribulation Rapture.* Denver, Colorado: Accent Books, 1980.

Bell, William E. A Critical Evaluation of the Pretribulation Rapture Doctrine in Christian Eschatology. Ph. D. dissertation, NYU, 1967.

Bock, Darrell. "Why I Am a Dispensationalist With a Small "d" *Journal of the Evangelical Theological Society* 41/3 (September 1998), 383-398.

---------------and Craig Blaising. *Progressive Dispensationalism.* Bridgepoint Books, 1993.

Calvin, John. *Calvin's Commentaries Vol. XXI.* Grand Rapids: Baker, 1979 reprint.

Chafer, Lewis Sperry. *Systematic Theology IV.* Dallas, Texas: Dallas Seminary Press, 1948.

-------------- and John F. Walvoord. *Major Bible Themes.* Grand Rapids: Zondervan, 1974.

Couch, Mal, ed. *A Biblical Theology of the Church.* Grand Rapids: Kregel, 1999.

Ellicott, Charles John. *Commentary on the Epistles of St. Paul to the Thessalonians.* Grand Rapids: Zondervan, 1957 reprint.

English, E. Schuyler. "Rethinking the Rapture," *Our Hope* 56 (May 1950) 650-666.

Erickson, Millard J. A Basic Guide to Eschatology: Making Sense of the Millennium. Grand Rapids: Baker Books, 1998.

Feinberg, Paul D. "The Case for Pre-Tribulationism" in *The Rapture: Pre-, Mid-, or Post-Tribulational.* Grand Rapids: Zondervan Academie Books, 1984.

Frykholm, Amy Johnson. *Rapture Culture: Left Behind in Evangelical America.* New York: Oxford University Press, 2004.

Fuller, Daniel P. *The Hermeneutics of Dispensationalism.* Chicago, Illinois: Northern Baptist Theological Seminary, diss. 1957, copyright 1966.

Gaebelein, A. C. *The Olivet Discourse.* Grand Rapids: Baker, 1969.

Gerstner, John H. *Wrongly Dividing the Word of Truth.* Brentwood, Tennessee: Woglemuth and Hyatt Publishers, 1991.

Gibben, Crawford. *Rapture Fiction.* Darlington, England: Evangelical Press, 2006.

Gundry, Robert H. *The Church and the Tribulation.* Grand Rapids: Zondervan, 1973.

*Since I have found agreement with Gundry's eschatological work found in this book, I should note my disappointment and disagreement with some of his later work regarding inerrancy and justification.

Hamilton, Floyd E. The Basis of Millennial Faith. Grand Rapids: Eerdmans, 1942.

Hendriksen, William. New Testament Commentary: Thessalonians. Grand Rapids: Baker, 1979.

Hiebert, D. Edmond. *The Thessalonian Epistles.* Chicago: Moody Press, 1971.

Ice, Thomas and Timothy Demy. *Prophecy Watch.* Eugene, Oregon: Harvest House Publishers, 1998.

---------------"The Marriage Supper of the Lamb" http://www.pretrib.org/data/pdf/Ice-TheMarriageSupperoft.pdf

Katterjohn, Arthur D. with Mark Fackler. *The Tribulation People.* Carol Stream, Illinois: Creation House, 1975.

Kimbro, Reginald C. *The Gospel According to Dispensationalism.* Toronto: Wittenburg Publications, 1995.

Ladd, George Eldon. *The Blessed Hope.* Grand Rapids: Eerdmans, 1956.

---------------*The Revelation of John.* Grand Rapids: Eerdmans, 1972.

Lindsay, Hal with C. C. Carlson. *The Late Great Planet Earth.* Grand Rapids: Zondervan, 1970.

MacArthur, John. *The MacArthur Study Bible.* Nashville, Tennessee: Word Publishing, 1997.

Matthison, Keith. *Dispensationalism: Rightly Dividing the People of God?* Philipsburg, New Jersey: Presbyterian and Reformed, 1995.

Mayhue, Richard. "Why a Pretribulational Rapture?" *The Master's Seminary Journal* 13/2 (Fall 2002), 241-253.

Moo, Douglas J., et.al. *The Rapture: Pre-, Mid-, or Post-Tribulational.* Grand Rapids: Zondervan Academie Books, 1984.

Mounce, Robert H. *The Book of Revelation (*Grand Rapids: Eerdmans, 1977).

Murray, Iain. *The Puritan Hope.* Edinburgh: Banner of Truth, 1971.

Murray, John. *The Epistle to the Romans.* Grand Rapids: Eerdmans, 1959.

Newton, B. W. *Prospects of the Ten Kingdoms of the Roman Empire.* Essex, England: n.d. Sovereign Grace Advent Testimony, Reprint, Fourth Edition.

Nichols, S. J. "The Dispensational View of the DavidicKingdom: A Response to ProgressiveDispensationalism" *The Master's Seminary Journal* 7 (1996), 213- 239.

Osborn, Grant T. Baker Exegetical Commentary on the New Testament: Revelation. Grand Rapids: Baker Academic, 2002.

Oxford Dictionary of English. Oxford University Press, 2009.

Payne, J. Barton. *The Theology of the Older Testament.* Grand Rapids: Zondervan, 1962.

Pentecost, J. Dwight. *Things to Come.* Grand Rapids: Zondervan Academie Books, 1964.

Reese, Alexander. *The Approaching Advent of Christ.* Grand Rapids: Grand Rapids International Publications, 1975 reprint.

Reiter, Richard R. "The Development of the Rapture Positions" in *The Rapture: Pre- Mid- or Post-Tribulational?* Grand Rapids: Zondervan Acadamie Books, 1984.

Riddlebarger, Kim. *The Man of Sin.* Grand Rapids: Baker, 2006.

Rosenthal, Marvin. *The Pre-Wrath Rapture of the Church.* Nashville, Tennessee: Thomas Nelson Publishers, 1990.

Ryrie, Charles Caldwell. *Basic Theology.* Chicago: Moody Press, 1999.

--------------*Dispensationalism Today.* Chicago: Moody Press, 1965.

--------------*Dispensationalism.* Chicago: Moody Press, 1995, revised and expanded.

---------------*Basis of the Premillennial Faith.* Neptune, New Jersey: Loizeaux Brothers, 1983.

---------------*First and Second Thessalonians.* Chicago: Moody Press, 1959.

---------------*Revelation.* Chicago: Moody Press, 1968.

Saucy, Robert. *The Case for Progressive Dispensationalism.* Grand Rapids: Zondervan, 1993.

Schaff, Philip. *History of the Christian Church,* 8 vols. Grand Rapids: Eerdmans, 1985.

Schreiner, Thomas R. *New Testament Theology.* Grand Rapids: Baker Academic, 2008.

Smith, J. B. *A Revelation of Jesus Christ.* Scottdale, Pennsylvania: Herald Press, 1961.

Stanton, Gerald. *Kept From the Hour.* Grand Rapids: Zondervan, 1956.

Stott, John R. W. *The Message of 1 & 2 Thessalonians.* Downers Grove, Illinois: Intervarsity Press, 1991.

Thiessen, Henry Clarence, revised by Vernon Doerksen. *Lectures in Systematic Theology.* Grand Rapids: Eerdmans, 1979.

Thomas, Robert L. *Revelation 1-7: An Exegetical Commentary.* Chicago: Moody Press, 1992.

Tregelles, Samuel P. *Remarks on the Prophetic Visions of Daniel.* London: Sovereign Grace Advent Testimony, 1965. Reprinted from Samuel Bagster and Sons M.DCCC.LXIV.

Walvoord, John F. *The Rapture Question.* Grand Rapids: Zondervan, 1957.

---------------*The Thessalonian Epistles.* Grand Rapids: Zondervan, 1967.

Wolff, Richard. *General Epistles of First and Second Thessalonians.* Wheaton, Illinois: Tyndale House, 1970.

18360811R00105

Printed in Great Britain
by Amazon